U.S. Education Is in Trouble, Let's Fix It!

U.S. Education Is in Trouble, Let's Fix It!

22 Reform Proposals

Richard W. Garrett

ROWMAN & LITTLEFIELD
Lanham • Boulder • New York • London

Published by Rowman & Littlefield
An imprint of The Rowman & Littlefield Publishing Group, Inc.
4501 Forbes Boulevard, Suite 200, Lanham, Maryland 20706
www.rowman.com

86-90 Paul Street, London EC2A 4NE, United Kingdom

British Library Cataloguing in Publication Information Available

Library of Congress Cataloging-in-Publication Data

Names: Garrett, Richard W., 1939– author.
Title: U.S. education is in trouble, let's fix it! : 22 reform proposals / Richard W. Garrett.
Other titles: United States education is in trouble, let's fix it!
Description: Lanham, Maryland : Rowman & Littlefield, 2023. | Includes bibliographical
    references and index. | Summary: "The scope of this book is the reform of the
    U.S. public education system. The theme is to find those things that are blocking
    improvements and to recommend solutions"— Provided by publisher.
Identifiers: LCCN 2023016445 (print) | LCCN 2023016446 (ebook) | ISBN
    9781475872460 (cloth) | ISBN 9781475872477 (paperback) | ISBN
    9781475872484 (epub)
Subjects: LCSH: Educational change—United States. | School improvement programs—
    United States. | Public schools—United States.
Classification: LCC LA217.2 .G369 2023 (print) | LCC LA217.2 (ebook) | DDC
    371.2/070973—dc23/eng/20230418
LC record available at https://lccn.loc.gov/2023016445
LC ebook record available at https://lccn.loc.gov/2023016446

♾™ The paper used in this publication meets the minimum requirements of American
National Standard for Information Sciences—Permanence of Paper for Printed Library
Materials, ANSI/NISO Z39.48-1992.

Contents

Preface

"Dick, get a good education, it is the very best thing you can do for yourself and your family. It is something nobody can ever take away from you; it is an investment that will inflate with inflation. In addition, it will set the stage for 'life-long learning,' an essential ingredient in today's fast-changing world."

How many times did I hear this as I was growing up from my father who was a small-town attorney? He earned his living by his wits; he had to know things, or how to find things, to be an effective lawyer. The fact that he earned a degree in law is itself remarkable. Here's his story:

Harvey W. Garrett was born on a watermelon farm in Patoka, Indiana, in 1901. He had three brothers and a father who was ill with tuberculosis. His father was in a sanitarium in Detroit but when Harvey was 14 his father surprisingly showed up at the farm; he had come home to die. Mother, Lou Garrett, carried on with the farm and remarried sometime later. She was severely injured in a farm accident while using a team of mules to remove a tree stump and died several months later in 1918. Her death dissolved the family and my father headed for Detroit; he was 18 and a small-town farm boy.

While in Detroit he worked several jobs but wanted to travel, so he became a hobo, begging for food and traveling the country sleeping in freight cars and dodging railroad detectives. He ended up as the hired hand for a wheat farmer in Saskatchewan, Canada. (Why did he go north? Why not sunny California?) His farmer boss was a good man, and he talked my father into saving up money so he could travel back to Indiana and get a college education. This he did, earning a degree in law from Indiana University. He went on to set up a law practice in the small town of Princeton, Indiana.

Later in life, the governor appointed him the judge of Gibson County, Indiana. He always wanted to die "with his boots on" and this he did at the age of 75 while still serving on the bench.

My father's words and life example had a profound impact on my life, my interests, and my accomplishments. I earned two degrees in engineering and a PhD in operations research (applied math). This was very much his doing.

Currently, I am totally committed to working to reform the U.S. public school PreK-12 education system. I want others to find their way out of poverty using the education road the way my father did.

Here's my story of how and why I became involved in education reform. This is text taken from my previous book[1], *The Kids Are Smart Enough, So What's the Problem? A Businessman's Perspective on Educational Reform and the Teacher Crisis*, detailing how I became involved in education reform. The text below is taken from chapter 1 of the book.

Daily Phone Calls

The phone rings. It is late in the afternoon and, as happens many days, it is son John calling after a day at school; he is on his way home and he needs to talk. In the early part of his 16-year teaching career, he did not make these phone calls; these past few years, they've become very regular and, unfortunately, they aren't uplifting calls as he describes what happened in his school that day.

Frustration about not being able to control the classroom or not getting assistance from parents or the administration fuels his discontent. His job is to change lives and he is not getting enough real teaching time to make much difference in these children's lives. He does not only share about just his fourth-grade classroom, but about all the fourth-grade classrooms and often other grades as well.

Today he had to restrain a child going through a tantrum that lasted 14 minutes.

"Can you actually restrain a child?" I ask. "You can if you do it the approved way," he says.

He and his colleagues realized that not much happens when you send a disruptive student to the office, so the four fourth-grade teachers developed a plan that takes the main office out of the picture. The teachers deal with discipline issues in their rooms by sending misbehaving students to another one of the fourth-grade rooms. Imagine working hard to establish a "learning environment" and in pops a teacher with a child they could not manage asking if the student can sit in your class for a while. Or maybe you have a student who is out of control one day, so you simply send them to a different classroom for an hour. Is this good discipline?

In another call, he points out that the teachers have lost all their leverage in terms of benefits they can withhold from misbehaving children. For example, they are not allowed to take away recess, one of the few remaining options they had. So, the teachers organized misbehaving students into groups who "walked laps" around the play area to use up all the recess time, until a district official saw the students walking laps and chastised the principal for allowing this punishment.

He talks about profane outbursts, students fighting in the middle of a class, and disruptions to group activities to the point that teachers can no longer count on group activities to break the teaching pattern. Phone calls to parents seeking their assistance are often anything but productive. "He's at school; he's your problem." Over time, the bad classroom events relayed in these calls cover a wide range of very *demeaning* and *demoralizing* events for the teachers.

The teachers are in a difficult situation and there is little they can do about it. They have very little recourse and as adults they wonder why they must put up with this environment. As will be discussed later, more and more teachers are opting out of education.

A teacher like John, with an undergraduate degree in psychology, a degree in elementary education and a master's degree in psychology ought to be able to effectively manage his students. In addition, he is a fitness advocate who is about six foot four inches tall and has completed a half iron-man marathon. None of this seems to matter much; in his situation, there are too many factors against him for him to meet his objective of changing lives for the better.

Soon after the publication of the first book, son John, just like so many other teachers, resigned from teaching. He is happily situated in another job and has no desire to return to the classroom though he does admit he misses the children.

As for me, being much older and wiser about our public K-12 education systems, I am able to see its many shortcomings as well as possible solutions to remedy some of its problems. My passion is to promote a thorough reform of the public schools; I will do my best in this book to explain why and how to do this.

My interaction with son John and other teachers, and the damming performance of our students are strong motivating forces to "keep me in the game." This is just one more force that elevates my perseverance.

A Debt to Pay

Northwestern University granted me a PhD in operations research in 1968. Northwestern is a first-class institution that, by any measure, is an expensive college to attend. Fortunately, I was awarded a NASA fellowship that gave me a full ride for three years. The fellowship came with no stipulations or expectations as to what field I might enter. I am thankful to the American people for my advanced education, but I have always felt a need to generate some sort of "payback" to show my appreciation.

After all, I do not believe the American people paid for my degree to make my life better; they expect something in return, an invention, a new business, or something. Whether this book will add value to the national discussion on education is yet to be seen but it is an attempt to settle my assumed debt.

A family friend, Audwynn Newman, is a former cartoonist for Marvel and DC, as well as a concept artist for DreamWorks and Sony pictures. I asked him to utilize his skills to help tell the story of U.S. education. He did several panels, but figure P.1 is my favorite.

Those of us who study the education system are worried about not only the system, but about America as well. President Obama stated it this way in 2009:[2]

> The relative decline of American education is untenable for our economy, unsustainable for our democracy, and unacceptable for our children, and we cannot afford to let it continue.

One of my favorite sayings about education is, "The more you know, the worse it gets." The public's overall impression of our K-12 education is not good; if you take a deep dive into education, it is worse than the public imagines.

Figure P.1.   Breakdown of U.S. Education System

In this book, I discuss some of my observations about the educational system. Here is my statement of purpose:

> I am not sure we can raise the scores of our most disadvantaged students to a level equal to the outstanding countries, but I am sure we can do much, much better with these children. We can do so well that it will change our society for the better. More independent lives for these citizens, fewer incarcerations, less dependence on government programs and a swelling sense of pride, not just for them but the entire nation. Education is the only path out of poverty.

Richard W. Garrett

NOTES

1. Garrett, Richard W., *The Kids Are Smart Enough, So What's the Problem? A Businessman's Perspective on Educational Reform and the Teacher Crisis.* Rowman & Littlefield, 2017.

2. Speech to the Hispanic Chamber of Commerce on Education, American Rhetoric, March 9, 2009, https://www.americanrhetoric.com/speeches/barackobama/barack obamahispanicchamberofcommerce.htm

Acknowledgments

Writing a book is a major task and would be a bigger challenge if it weren't for helpers.

First and foremost is my wife, Bonnie Garrett. As a former teacher she has been a great advisor regarding the book's content. She also willingly supports the time I spend in research and writing.

Son John Garrett, a former elementary teacher who has been a vital resource on many things at many times. His teacher wife, Angel Garrett, has also been a great resource.

Laurie Abell, our daughter who proofed the final draft. She is good at it, and it gives me great comfort to know she has reviewed the book.

Audwynn Jermaine Newman did the cartoon in the preface. He was, at one time, a professional cartoonist.

Former astronaut Mark Brown and his wife Lynn were helpful on the design of the cover. They motivated a new chapter, chapter 16, National Impact.

Fabrice Decaudin is an active school principal and has provided good counsel and insights.

Thanks to Dana Scott for his professional work on all tables and figures.

So many others helped and supported me throughout this process. Marty Hollingsworth, our neighbor and former partner in a large Indianapolis law firm, has been a staunch supporter of my work and a vital resource in the legal area. As would be expected, she gives good counsel. Ms. Katie Browning has played a significant role in my website and social media. She always "adds value" to what she does.

Introduction

The quality of schooling in a country is a reliable predictor of the wealth that country will produce in the long run.

This book wants to plant the above quotation in every American's mind. This quote is from Andreas Schleicher[1] PhD, head of the Programme for International Student Assessment (PISA). As a nation we are participating in the world's biggest competition: to create wealth for our country. To do this, the country needs its citizens to cultivate great ideas and have the production capabilities to put those ideas into action. As a nation we still produce great ideas, but our labor force is lacking in skilled people to implement them.

Is this another book complaining about U.S. public education? Yes, it is. But it's different in that it will also focus on solutions to many of the problems. It is intended to provide the necessary background about the main issues and explain what needs to be done to fix those issues. Sometimes the fix is not expensive, requiring only policy or legislative changes. Sometimes the recommended approaches will be very expensive.

So, what is the goal?

The goal is an education system that will educate more children, educate them well, and put the United States in the top tier worldwide.

A Champion for the Children Who Come to School to Learn

This book is a champion for children who want to learn and for teachers who want to teach. How many children go to school each day hoping to learn? Most children have a strong desire to learn or at least are not opposed to it. In other words, under the right circumstances, these latter children will do just fine. As champions, this book wants to provide an environment where learning takes place. Please note, this book does not discuss the issue of the difficult home lives of many of our children. It becomes an important consideration when children are selected for entering school at 3 years of age.

This book separates children into three kinds of students.

1. Engaged learners clearly want to be good students and they work hard to learn.
2. Followers can go either way—become engaged students or become disruptive.
3. Disruptive students have no interest in learning and seem to go out of their way to make sure the other students don't learn either. These students often influence the behavior of the followers.

The disruptive students are the "bad apples" who ruin the class for the others. They obviously have no interest in learning and seem to go out of their way to make sure many of the other students don't learn as well.

Here's the reality; the few "bad apples" are ruining the entire barrel. Fix this problem and the system is much better. Listen to this research result, if the test scores of private school students are compared to the public schools, the private school test scores are better. Now, select the public-school kids whose backgrounds match up with the private school students, that is, compare apples to apples.

To do this use only grades of public-school students with similar socioeconomic backgrounds are considered. In this comparison, the reading scores are slightly lower, and the math scores are the same for the public students. So, the underlying public-school learning structure is just fine. To be successful ways need to be found to reduce some of the disadvantages of the public students. Parental influence is one factor and beginning to influence the children at age 3 is another.

Many Concerned about Education

There are millions of outstanding young students who truly want to learn. However, a few bad apples can spoil the entire basket. And everyone has a solution. For example, some people call for a return to corporal punishment. This worked in the past, so why not now? Others say the problem is the teachers; they are overpaid, their job is easy, and they can't control the kids.

Oh no, it's the parents, they don't pay enough attention to how their kids behave and they don't support the schools. Some people place all the blame on the young people. The kids these days don't care about learning. They don't respect anybody or anything. They are vulgar, crude, profane, disrespectful, and apathetic.

Clearly, the business of educating our children is fraught with accusations, excuses, and very little understanding.

Many do not fully understand how bad things can get in a school. An eye-opening video is available on my website, elevateteachers.org, that records the resignation of an award-winning teacher from the Green Bay, Wisconsin, school system. If you want to background yourself in some of the discipline and control issues go to the website elevateteachers.org, click on Lessons, and then click on Lesson 4. It is very distressing.

HOW MANY PEOPLE WORK IN ALL SCHOOLS?

To better understand the complexity of the business of educating our children, consider that the Bureau of Labor Statistics estimates that in May 2021, elementary and secondary schools employed more than 8 million people. That's more than twice as many workers as are employed in colleges, universities, and professional schools and over 400,000 more workers than are employed in the construction industry or in all retail sales jobs in the United States. It's also more than three times the number of employees in the real estate and rental and leasing industry. Elementary and secondary schools employ about two-thirds as many workers as the U.S. manufacturing industry. Figure I.1 is a graphic that makes this text a bit clearer, presented from the Riser-Kositsky[2] article.

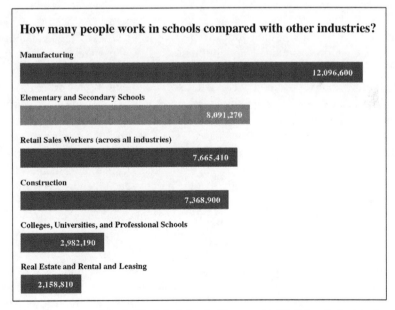

Figure I.1.   How Many People Work in Schools Compared with Other Industries?

Of those 8 million education employees, 66% work in educational instruction and library roles, including 3.6 million teachers and over 1 million teaching assistants. There were 3.6 million teachers working in preschools, elementary, middle, and high schools, and with special education students. About 350,000 people (about 4% of the school workforce) work in the management of schools, almost 500,000 (6%) work in administrative support, 330,000 (4%) work in building and grounds, and 315,000 (almost 4%) work in food preparation and service. Other occupations in schools, including transportation, health care, and financial operations, employ 1.2 million people, or over 15% of everyone working in schools.

There were almost 3% fewer teachers across all PreK grades in May 2021 than there were in May 2016, but salaries for teachers increased over 13% in that period. In May 2021, the Bureau of Labor Statistics reported teachers' annual mean wage as $67,680.

In addition, there are 97,600 public schools in the U.S., with approximately 13,880 school districts.[3] The world of PreK-12 education is a BIG business and this makes it all the harder to manage and control.

Can it possibly be reformed? There have been many attempts, and almost all have failed to make needed changes. What we need is an uproar from millions of American citizens, and the timing is right. Test scores continue to languish, even decline, and educators are leaving the profession in droves, leaving schools unable to provide properly trained personnel in the classrooms and in the front office.

Control from the national level, as we will discuss later, has not worked, and may do more harm than good. Well-established and accepted educational policy must be formulated and implemented at the state level. Teachers' unions may try to interfere; they must be brushed aside. Many of their past efforts have not supported educational excellence, but instead have inhibited progress. For example, the termination of an unproductive teacher can be a monumental problem.

As George Will wrote in the *Washington Post*[4] in 2016 regarding teacher tenure in California (which they were granted after just two years, according to Will), "When incompetent or negligent teachers gain tenure, dismissal procedures are so complex and costly that the process can take up to 10 years and cost up to $450,000. . . . Each year approximately two teachers are dismissed for unsatisfactory performance—.0007% of California's 277,000 teachers."

Rather than fighting for the tenure rights of incompetent teachers, the unions ought to be certifying teachers to be capable of delivering excellent teaching; they should be leading the charge to upgrade all public schools, but this is fairy dust. Instead, they go to elaborate ends to retain the worst teachers. This is unacceptable; the education ship is sinking and in need of repair. All hands should be laser focused on making those repairs.

We need a citizen's revolt that will demand that the United States be placed on the right track, the track to excellence. Our American values need to be rebooted to produce a system that will educate all citizens, a system that will produce citizens who are well-educated and prepared to assume their role in our society and economic structure.

Bringing Research to the People

Getting a firm hold on the issues and concerns takes a steady hand and lots of work. Hopefully, the material presented here will be relevant and interesting and prompt readers to do some research of their own. If the "big picture" is the focus, the story cannot go too far off track.

UNFOLDING THIS BOOK

Chapter 1 notes that President George H. Bush convened state governors to establish National Education Goals. Once the conference was over, these goals were placed on the shelf never to be revisited. For example, one goal says that the U.S. will be number one in math skills; actually, math skills are our worst performance area, and the country is in the bottom 25% of all countries.

Chapter 2 presents numerous metrics (measures) that do not reflect America in a good light. For example, students' poor results in math and reading are troubling. Twenty-five percent of U.S. high school graduates between the ages of 16 and 74 have the reading skills of a 10-year-old. America's math skills are close to the bottom of the country list.

For decades, America was held up as the place where things were done right. This is no longer the case; the U.S. now sends delegates to foreign nations to see how they do so well.

Chapter 3 details the beginning of the decline in schools when, in the 1970s, adults were charged with ensuring no child experienced failure; the "every child gets a trophy" attitude.

Chapter 4 focuses on teachers: how many there are, what they are thinking, and what the future holds regarding supply and demand, among other topics.

Chapter 5 points out each day a teacher only has a limited number of "instructional minutes." It is of vital importance that they be given this time to teach. Discipline issues, events arising from not touching a child, attending to children who have been assigned to their classrooms who do not speak English, and so forth, erode this time.

Chapter 6 says discipline and lack of respect are tearing our schools apart. Much instructional time is wasted disciplining children. Lack of respect is making the teacher ask, "Why must I put up with this? I'm quitting." These two forces, along with low pay and poor management are driving more and more people away from U.S. classrooms.

Chapter 7 points out a successful student has two kinds of skills: cognitive (knowledge and thinking skills) and noncognitive, character and grit or social emotional learning.

Chapter 8 explains how schools should be organized. This chapter focuses on the four tracks that must be established to maximize individual student success. Unlike a naval military convoy that must travel at the speed of the slowest ship, schools should organize several tracts that will allow some students to forge ahead much more rapidly. Students in top international schools complete a high school education in 10 years, while U.S schools take 12 years and ofttimes, as will be shown in chapter 2, fail to do a good job.

Chapter 9 is a key chapter. Reading is by far the most important academic skill a person can possess. We in America do not do a very good job of teaching children how to read properly by the end of the third grade. Most of the time, students are promoted into the fourth grade regardless of their reading ability and will forever more be weak readers. We must do a better job teaching reading.

Chapter 10 explains some children must begin their formal education when they are 3 years old. Many students from more affluent families will receive the proper brain stimulation at home. Unfortunately, for many reasons, lower income parents do not have the skills or the time to provide proper brain stimulation. These are the children, and only these, who should begin school at age 3. They should develop a familiarity with books as their journey in reading begins. In addition, at this time they should be exposed to habits of behavior that will continue for several years. Saying yes sir and no mam, thank you, and so forth is a capability they can learn.

Chapter 11 asks, "Who's going to fix our system? Who's going to take the leadership role in reforming our system?" It is not going to come from the world of education; they have grown accustomed to disruptive children and poor test scores and do not exhibit leadership that will correct the many problems. On the other hand, businesspeople have a strong vested interest. They ask, "Where are we going to find our future workers?"

Chapter 12 elaborates on the legal issues that are a plague in the school systems.

Chapter 13 discusses teacher labor unions and how they are a strong force in the world of education, a force strong enough to thwart changes. Labor unions are respected adversaries with good people, and well-established power. America needs them to refocus this power on improving the system rather than destroying it.

Chapter 14 presents two case studies. The first details the monumental reforms made to the Massachusetts school systems in the early 1990s. These changes pushed the state to the number one position in the nation. They remain there today. Maryland is at the beginning of a major reform program. Some of the features of this program will be discussed.

Chapter 15 explains school system overhead is not often discussed. This chapter will highlight overhead as wasteful and as a diversion of funds away from the classroom.

Chapter 16 outlines the national impact of an excellent education system. It explains there is the very good return on investment from investing in education. The return for Maryland is $2.20 for every dollar spent on education. The chapter also enumerates intangible benefits from a strong education system.

Chapter 17 is the essence of this book, focusing on what are the major problems and what can be done about them. It highlights many issues and discusses how many can be fixed.

NOTES

1. Dr. Andreas Schleicher, PhD, is the head of the Program for International Student Assessment (PISA). He is the most knowledgeable person in the world on how various countries line up in the quality of their education system.

2. Riser-Kositsky, Maya, "How Many People Work in Schools and How Much Do They Get Paid?," *Education Week*, July 8, 2022, https://www.edweek.org/leadership/school-staffing-by-the-numbers/2022/06

3. Ballotpedia, https://ballotpedia.org/Public_school_district_(United_States)

4. Will, George, "The Injustice of California's Teacher Tenure," *Washington Post*, July 13, 2016, https://www.washingtonpost.com/opinions/undoing-the-harm-of-californias-teacher-tenure/2016/07/13/ec56dd90-484b-11e6-bdb9-701687974517_story.html

Chapter 1

Does the U.S. Have National Goals?

The United States is a "middle of the pack" performer in its K-12 academic performance when compared to other nations. Before looking at the data, it's beneficial to consider if the country has a national goal for education as it strives to move up in the international rankings.

WHAT IS THE U.S. EDUCATIONAL GOAL?

There is, in fact, a law that spells out the goals for U.S. education. Here is a summary of our national goals:

> At an education summit held in 1989, President George H. Bush and every state governor agreed upon 6 national education goals for the United States to achieve by the year 2000. Two more goals were added in 1994, and Congress passed legislation known as the National Education Goals.[1]

The National Educational Goals to be achieved by the year 2000 are:

1. All children in the United States will start school ready to learn.
2. The high school graduation rate will increase to at least 90%.
3. U.S. students will leave grades 4, 8, and 12 having demonstrated competency in challenging subject matters, including English, mathematics, science, foreign languages, civics and government, economics, arts, history, and geography; every school will ensure that all students learn to use their minds well, so they may be prepared for responsible citizenship, further learning, and productive employment in our nation's modern economy.
4. The nation's teaching force will have access to programs for the continued improvement of their professional skills and the opportunity

1

to acquire the knowledge and skills needed to instruct and prepare all students for the next century.

5. U.S. students will be first in the world in mathematics and science achievement.

6. Every adult American will be literate and will possess the knowledge and skills necessary to compete in a global economy and to exercise the rights and responsibilities of citizenship.

7. Every school in the United States will be free of alcohol and other drugs, violence, and the unauthorized presence of firearms and will offer a disciplined environment conducive to learning.

8. Every school will promote partnerships that will increase parental involvement and participation in promoting the social, emotional, and academic growth of children.

The Goals 2000: Educate America Act codified the goals and established federal support for voluntary, state-based systemic reform. These include the development and implementation of high academic standards.

Unfortunately, the U.S. has missed these goals by miles and miles. Look at them one by one.

1. All children in the United States will start school ready to learn.

The exposure and stimulation each child receives in their early years varies dramatically. Many students are well prepared for school, walking through the kindergarten door having already learned letters and numbers. Many low-income students enter school with minimal exposure to books or numbers. To address this lack of early education, many countries have developed programs for low-income students that begin their education at age 3. This is not the case for the United States.

2. The high school graduation rate will increase to at least 90%.

Many states are already near 90% graduation rate, according to their website. Yet, the "actual" graduation rate is often lower because students who have not met the published requirements, such as passing a math test, receive a waiver to the full diploma. Given that 25% of U.S. high school graduates have the reading skills of a 10-year-old, it's hard to imagine how in the world they were granted a diploma.

3. U.S. students will leave grades 4, 8, and 12 having demonstrated competency in challenging subject matters, including English, mathematics, science, foreign languages, civics and government, economics, arts, history, and geography; every school will ensure that all students learn to use their minds well, so they may be prepared for responsible citizenship, further learning, and productive employment in our nation's modern economy.

The next chapter will show the fact that this goal has not been met, not even close.

4. The nation's teaching force will have access to programs for the continued improvement of their professional skills and the opportunity to acquire the knowledge and skills needed to instruct and prepare all students for the next century.

   A critical teacher shortage is coming that will stress the entire system. Schools currently are "grabbing people off the street" and putting them in the classroom.

5. U.S. students will be first in the world in mathematics and science achievement.

   In the assessment of high school graduates in adult competency (a sample of citizens in the 16–72 age range), the United States ranks 22/32 (22nd out of 32 countries) in our citizens' ability to solve simple math problems. Looking at problem solving in a digital environment (use of computers), U.S. citizens rank 11/25 with 33% of the people unable to solve a simple problem using the computer. The science rank comes from student testing under the PISA (Program for International Assessment). The U.S. rank is 15/80. The United States is a long way from first place.

6. Every adult American will be literate and will possess the knowledge and skills necessary to compete in a global economy and to exercise the rights and responsibilities of citizenship.

   It has already been pointed out that 25% of our 16- to 72-year-olds cannot read beyond the level of a 10-year-old child. Other measures, to be discussed in the next chapter, are also discouraging.

No comment will be made regarding success on items 7 and 8.

Whatever forces were at play to define these goals back in 1989 have quickly dissipated since the United States is factually now headed in the wrong direction regarding reading. Most Americans have never heard about the Educate America Act. Why can't we Americans take the step to reform this system? So far, it's all just talk.

SIMPLE GOAL

Clearly, the country needs major reform and a simple goal: 80% of all high school graduates become college or career ready by the end of 2035.

America's Education Goal—Attain 80% CCR by 2035

This will be a stretch goal. The list of things needing to change to achieve this goal is long and complicated.

NOTE

1. U.S. Legal website, http://education.uslegal.com/curriculum/national-education -goals

Chapter 2

U.S. Students Are Not as Good as We Think

This chapter presents academic performance results that will demonstrate the fact that the U.S. is a "middle of the pack" performer. A disappointing aspect of these results is the fact that the U.S. spends 35% more on education than the average of the developed nations. In other words, we are spending more and getting less.

Amidst the negative information about the country's public education system, there is some good news to report. The news comes from Bill Gates and his foundation. They have spent enormous sums of money working to improve U.S. public education for many years.

Here's what Gates reports:

> For years, the top 20% of U.S. students are as good and many times better that the top 20% in any other nation. They go to the best schools and universities and have driven our economy into the top ranks. This continues to be the case, but our economy has changed, and education must change with it.[1]

The jobs that are growing in America require a better trained student and as Mr. Gates points out, the remaining 80% of our population must be better prepared to keep the country competitive and growing.

HOW TO ASSESS STUDENTS TO DETERMINE WHAT THEY KNOW

Over the years there have been movements to eliminate both tests and letter grades. To some, exams are considered mean because they make the test taker look incapable or unfit in the aftermath. It is difficult to deal with a bad grade, especially if the grades are not private. Is this enough of an issue that tests should be outlawed? Let us hope not, good grades are rewards for extra

5

effort and commitment; bad grades are a punishment for either not working hard enough or perhaps for not applying one's brain power.

A couple phrases come to mind when it comes to testing:

1. From industry: It's not what you expect; it's what you inspect.
2. From international weapons control: trust but verify.

In education, some kind of measure is required to verify performance; the customary practice usually relies on a test.

The bottom line here is that human nature being what it is, some need a hammer over their heads to motivate higher levels of performance. Many are inherently looking for ways to avoid work, to find an easy way out. Learning is hard work and there is no way around it.

How Are Students to Be Evaluated?

Many students do not make the kind of commitment to pursue the work needed to obtain a good grade. *Students who don't know the material do not do well on exams.* Top students want the good grades and are highly motivated to put in the needed work. They highly value a good test score, because to them the competition is in the classrooms; this is the scoreboard for this competitive game. They want to win!

There are many people who are opposed to using tests and even grades to judge students. A recent article pointed out that the way to reduce the racial gap is to quit testing! This might result in apparent equity, but it certainly doesn't help in setting up methods to close the gap.

How Do U.S. Students Perform?

The nation's public schools use a variety of measures that tell us what students *do*, not what they know. Metrics range from graduation rates to suspension rates, from school attendance to student-teacher ratios. There is an underlying assumption in these numbers that students absorb a sound base of knowledge as they travel through their PK-12 journey. This assumption is completely inaccurate for many children.

The most disappointing evidence comes from the assessment of adult competencies. The Program for the International Assessment of Adult Competencies, PIAAC, is a cyclical, large-scale study developed under the auspices of the Organization for Economic Cooperation and Development (OECD). It is a well-established measurement system used across the globe in 38 countries. In the most recent 2017/2018 study, they assessed a sample of the U.S. pool of 16- to 74-year-olds.

Thirty-eight countries participated in this study but due to the resolution of ties, less than 38 countries are shown in the rankings.

In literacy, 25% (52 million) have the reading skills of a 10-year-old, placing America 12th among 29 nations measured. (Recall a high score is bad.) This dismal level of verbal competence was 20% in the program's previous 2012 study, so the reading situation has gotten worse by 5 points.[2]

In numerical competence, 38% (79 million) of Americans lack basic math-related skills. The U.S. ranks 22nd among 32 nations. The U.S. "numeracy" shortfall has deepened; the previous level in this category was 33%.[3]

An assessment of "problem-solving in a digital environment" found 33% (69 million) to be digitally incompetent, up from the 30% level the program reported in 2012. Currently, the U.S. ranks 11th among 25 nations.[4]

This "getting worse" trend in their findings should be alarming to us all.

Additional Data Shows More Concerning Insights

Compared to similar age groups in the developed world, the 67 million U.S. millennials (now 25–40 years old) are the least well-educated. This result is drawn from competency testing.[5] A 2015 article in *The Atlantic* summarizes:

> As a country, we need to address the question of whether we can afford . . . to write off nearly half of our younger-adult population as not having the skills needed to effectively engage as full and active participants in their own future and that of our nation.

Student Reading and Math Abilities Flat for Forth–Eight Years

Here is information from the NAEP website that explains their role and organization.

> The National Assessment of Educational Progress (NAEP) provides important information about student achievement and learning experiences in various subjects. Also known as The Nation's Report Card, NAEP has provided meaningful results to improve education policy and practice since 1969. Results are available for the nation, states, and 27 urban districts.
>
> NAEP is a congressionally mandated program that is overseen and administered by the National Center for Education Statistics (NCES), within the U.S. Department of Education and the Institute of Education Sciences. The National Assessment Governing Board, an independent body appointed by the Secretary of Education, sets NAEP policy.[6]

In 1970, the National Assessment of Educational Progress (NAEP) began a long-term analysis of student performance in several areas. Reading and math data from The Nation's Report Card[7] spanning 48 years are illustrated in figure 2.1.[8]

Do these graphs show any true growth? Is it possible to draw a straight line with an upward trend that is statistically meaningful? The data points were placed in an Excel spreadsheet and a statistically calculated trend line was generated for each. The result of this analysis is given here.

Reading Scores (the top graph): This shows 48 years of data and in those 48 years there was a 20-point growth in reading test scores for 9-year-olds. There is an average .42 points per year in reading scores. Statistically speaking, the 9-year-old graph shows some real growth, but it is very slow. It takes 82 years to improve by 10% over the year 2020 value, a score of 220. The score growth in the 13-year-old reading graph is not statistically significant, in other words, it's flat, so there is never any predicable improvement in their performance. It only grew five points in 48 years.

Math Scores: Both math lines, 9-year-olds and 13-year-olds, are statistically flat; there has been no real growth in math scores in 48 years.

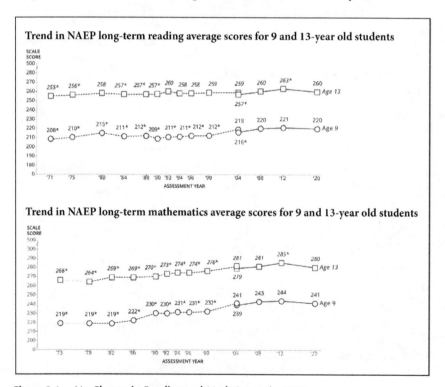

Figure 2.1.   No Change in Reading and Math Scores in 48 Years

Government Programs

Stepping back and looking at the big picture, these "flat" results have persisted during a period of dramatic construction of state and federal bureaucracies, new laws, the creation of many different teaching approaches and assessment exams, attacks on the educational system by the press, and much blame heaped upon teachers. The lack of improvement in student performance leads to the conclusion that none of the programs worked, all wasted money.

All this superstructure could well be part of the problem. Bureaucracies have a way of creating work that will justify their existence. The teachers complain about all the extra paperwork they must generate to satisfy these requests. Quite obviously extreme corrective action should be attempted, and efforts need to be made to engage the teachers in the solutions.

The PISA Assessment System

Finally, the results of the Programme for International Student Assessment (PISA) are the most influential in ranking U.S. students relative to their peers in more than 77 countries around the world.

Every three years the PISA survey provides comparative data on 15-year-old's performance in reading, mathematics, and science in developed countries affiliated with the Organization for Economic Co-operation and Development (OECD). The countries are divided into two groups: those with full membership in OECD and those affiliated but not full members.

Here is the 2018 ranking data for the United States.[9] These results may vary from other reports because, rather than count the U.S. position in a list of 35 countries, this analysis first removes ties by allowing multiple countries to occupy the same line in the list. All the presented results are created this way. Both ranks are presented but in the ensuing discussion on the full member OECD rankings are evaluated.

Reading: The U.S. ranks 7/28 in the OECD, the only list placing them in the top 25% of countries. In the all-country list, the U.S. ranks 11/62 or in the top 18%.

Mathematics: The U.S. ranks 23/29 in the OECD only list or in the bottom 21%. The U.S. is 30/66 in the all-country, placing it in the bottom 55%.

Science: The U.S. ranks 10/29 in the OECD, the only list placing it in the top 34% of countries. It ranks 16/64 in the all-country list, placing it in the top 25% of all countries.

Where Should the U.S. Rank?

Where should the U.S. rank? The likely consensus answer to this question would be near the top. Every country wants the same thing. The reading position as a top 25% performer of all countries is the best showing of the three measures for the U.S. It was reported earlier in this chapter that 25% of U.S. high school graduates are poor readers..

This book is about making changes that will improve the U.S. ranking. One thing is for sure, it is not going to be easy to change the system; there have been many attempts and most all have failed. What is needed is a full population cry for improved education and legislative support to make the needed changes and funding. It will be expensive so finding funding is essential.

Don't Widen the Plate, Don't Lower Standards

Teachers and administrators may think they are doing their children a favor as they widen the plate in most everything they do. This is an example of "Everyone gets a trophy." Children are not falling for this strategy; they know that getting a trophy for just showing up is not worthy. If they didn't earn the honor, they place no value on having a trophy. As one looks at what makes a school successful, there is a strategy to set high standards and expect the children to perform at that level. If they don't perform, you pull them up and let the standards stand. There is an old saying, if you don't expect much that is exactly what you get.

Here are two examples of how schools are widening the plate. Grade inflation is running rampant according to data presented by The College Board,

In 1998, 38.9% of high schoolers had an "A" average. By 2016, the rate had increased to 47%. Meanwhile, the average SAT score fell from 1026 to 1002 on the 1600-point scale.[10]

A national survey shows when parents were asked if their children were performing at or above grade level, 90% said they were. But, in fact, only 34% were.

According to research[11] from Learning Heroes, 9 out of 10 parents of public-school students, regardless of race, income, and education level, believe their child is at or above grade level in reading and math. However, scores on the 8th grade National Assessment of Educational Progress (NAEP) in 2019, found that barely 34% of students are proficient in both math and reading.[12]

After all, their kids are bringing home "A's" so all must be well at school. Table 2.1 is an example of a grading scale that was featured on the TV show *Dr. Phil* on November 1, 2022. A parent sent this in and said it was the published scale for their child's school. It's dangerous to present something like

Table 2.1. School Grading Scale

School Grading Scale	
A	84 to 100%
B	64 to 84%
C	44 to 64%
D	24 to 44%
F	0 to 24%

this without firm knowledge that it is real, but its impact on grading is consistent with stories heard from teachers.

The only thing that is inconsistent is the failing grade of "F." Teachers report that their school will not allow an "F" grade for any reason. They will not fail a student even though they never show up for school. With grading schedules like this, it is easy to understand how 47% of the students have an "A" average.

Another example of "widening the plate" is the reduction of our historically high standards. This is the worst kind of corruption; it represents the debasing of what has been a pillar throughout the years of the U.S. education system. It undoubtedly is an overt strategy of schools to make themselves look better and to keep the heat off their inability to properly teach their children.

In 2014, a high school in Ohio awarded the honor of class valedictorian to 72 out of their graduating class of 222; the next year a Virginia high school awarded this title to 117 out of 457 graduates.

Are Private School Test Scores Better than Public Schools?

The quick answer is yes, but wait a minute! What happens when public-school children are selected to match the backgrounds of the private school students? Let's look.

Several recent large-scale studies have compared private schools to charter and regular public schools using the one common test taken by selected samples of students around the country.

That test is the National Assessment of Educational Progress (NAEP), otherwise known as the Nation's Report Card. Administered by the U.S. Department of Education, the NAEP is given to students in grades 4, 8, and 12 in both private and public schools.

One of these studies, conducted by Christopher and Sarah Theule Lubienski, a husband-and-wife team at the University of Illinois, compared more than 340,000 students using math scores from the 2003 NAEP. The report found that after adjusting for socioeconomic factors, there is little difference *between private and public-school scores.*

According to the researchers, "Demographic differences between students in public and private schools more than account for the relatively high raw scores of private schools. Indeed, after controlling for these differences, the presumably advantageous 'private school effect' disappears, and even reverses in most cases."

Similarly, another study: Comparing Private Schools and Public Schools Using Hierarchical Linear Modeling used the 2003 NAEP data. It found that after adjusting for student characteristics such as gender, race, ethnicity, disability status and English-language proficiency and for school characteristics such as size, location, and the makeup of the student body, the fourth-grade reading test scores were virtually the same for private and public schools, although the math scores for public schools were higher.

In eighth grade, private school students performed better in reading, but there was virtually no difference in math. When apples are compared to apples, the public schools do just fine; this is great and redeeming news. It lets us know that there are many students in our public schools who are receiving a good education. It brings home that our public schools are faced with the responsibility of welcoming all comers to their classes, each of whom have great value and each of whom needs to be properly educated.[13]

In summary, the U.S. public education system is charged with educating all students and in the process is producing mediocre results. It is far below where most Americans think it is and, in some areas, it is getting worse. With performance like what has been described, this country is not fielding enough well-trained students to be competitive in the world economic competition. This inevitably will move wealth away from our shores to foreign countries who produce top quality students.

Administrators have opted to "make the children" happy over the loftier goal of making our schools centers of excellence. Student happiness is fleeting; students need self-confidence, not happiness; giving away grades does not build self-confidence.

NOTES

1. Gates, Bill, transcription of video, https://www.youtube.com/watch?v =OnfzZEREfQs

2. National Center for Educational Statistics, Highlights of PIAAC 2017 US Results, Figure 5B, https://nces.ed.gov/surveys/piaac/national_results.asp, the global ranking were derived from using data from all 38 countries on a spreadsheet.

3. Ibid.

4. Ibid.

5. Zinshteyn, Mikhil, "The Skills Gap: America's Young Workers Are Lagging Behind," *The Atlantic*, February 15, 2015, https://www.theatlantic.com/education/archive/2015/02/the-skills-gap-americas-young-workers-are-lagging-behind/385560/

6. https://www.nationsreportcard.gov/ltt/?age=9

7. Ibid.

8. Wilde, Marian, "Apples and Oranges: Comparing Private and Public Test Scores," Great Schools, March 18, 2016, https://www.greatschools.org/gk/articles/comparing-private-public-school-test-scores/

9. OECDiLibrary, 2018 results, https://www.oecd-ilibrary.org/education/pisa-2018-results-volume-i_5f07c754-en;jsessionid=YDOFJTv1eLkOmFy62OIawWQcNQfzCyMKIuCzjcHR.ip-10-240-5-169

10. Weller, Chris, "There's an Epidemic of Grade Inflation and Unearned as in American High Schools," *Insider*, July 18, 2017, https://www.businessinsider.com/grade-inflation-us-high-schools-2017-7

11. No author given, "Do U.S. Parents Overestimate Their Student's Progress?," NCEE, 1/14/21, https://ncee.org/quick-read/do-u-s-parents-overestimate-their-students-progress/

12. "Do US Parents Overestimate Their Student's Progress?," *Top of the Class Newsletter*, *NCEE*, no date given, https://ncee.org/quick-read/do-u-s-parents-overestimate-their-students-progress/

13. Wilde, Marian, "Apples and Oranges: Comparing Private and Public Test Scores," Great Schools, March 18, 2016, https://www.greatschools.org/gk/articles/comparing-private-public-school-test-scores/

Chapter 3

When Did Things
Begin to Go Bad?

What are the "root causes" of the decline of the U.S. public-school system? One root cause is school administrators trying to elevate student self-esteem, but their actions are having the wrong effect. Giving undeserving students "A's" to boost their self-esteem actually can lower it. It takes away a sense of accomplishment, where a real "A" could build self-confidence.

A little story. Mom asks son Johnny to clean up his room. Later, as she walks by, she sees that he has two piles of his trophies on his bed. She asks, "Why two piles?" He points to the smaller pile and says, "These are the ones I earned, I'm keeping these." He points to the other, larger pile, and says "I am getting rid of those. I got those just because I participated. Everybody got one." He's no fool, he knows the difference. He is getting rid of the unearned rewards.

The last chapter reported on several similar deceptions. Forty-seven percent of US high school students have an "A" average; the real "A" students are deprived of the honor they worked hard to earn thus lowering their self-esteem and motivation. The remainder of the students received an honor they didn't deserve, lowering their self-esteem. Do not discount pride; build pride, don't tear it down. Just like Johnny in the story, they know the difference between earned and unearned.

Consider a Virginia high school that designated 117 of its 457 graduating seniors as valedictorians. This "kind" attempt to lift students debases the value of the award for everyone, especially the student(s) who truly earned the designation. For the students who were not traditionally deserving, this lowers their self-esteem since they have been played for a fool.

THE SELF-ESTEEM MOVEMENT

The psychotherapist Nathaniel Branden is often called the father of the self-esteem movement. He wrote the seminal book *The Psychology of Self-Esteem* in 1969 and the definitive book—*The Six Pillars of Self-Esteem*—in 1994.

Who can be against creating healthy self-esteem in anybody? The issue is how it's done. Here is an excerpt from an article titled: "Popular Culture: America's Self-Esteem Problem Rewarding Children No Matter What They Do Does Not Create Real Self-esteem." The title says it all, rewarding children no matter what they do does not create self-esteem.

> Self-esteem is commonly thought of as how we feel about ourselves, our appraisal of our own self-worth. But real self-esteem is a complex attribute that has become one of the most misunderstood and misused psychological characteristics of the last 40 years. Sometime back in the '70s when the "self-esteem movement" started, a bunch of parenting experts said that raising well-adjusted children is all about self-esteem. Most people would agree.
>
> This is also when America's self-esteem problem began because parents and other influences on self-esteem (e.g., teachers and coaches) got the wrong messages about self-esteem from those experts. Instead of creating children with true self-esteem, our country has created a generation of children who, for all the appearances of high self-esteem, have little regard for themselves (because they have little on which to base their self-esteem).
>
> Where did our society err in our failed attempts to build true self-esteem in our children? These same experts told parents that they could build their children's self-esteem by telling them how smart and talented and beautiful and incredible they were ("You're the best, Johnny!"). In other words, parents were led to believe that they could convince their children how wonderful they were.
>
> Unfortunately, life has a way of providing a reality check and children learned the hard way that they weren't as fabulous as their parents told them they were. Parents were also told to praise and reinforce and reward their children no matter what they did. The result: lower self-esteem and children who were self-centered and spoiled.
>
> Schools and communities accepted this misguided attempt at building self-esteem by "protecting" children from failure and feeling bad about themselves. For example, school grading systems were changed. I remember between sixth and seventh grade, my middle school replaced F for failure with NI (Needs Improvement); god forbid I'd feel bad about myself for failing at something!
>
> Youth sports made the same mistake. They eliminated scoring, winners, and losers in the belief that losing would hurt children's self-esteem. My 10-year-old niece came home one day from a soccer tournament with a ribbon that said "#1-Winner" on it. When I asked her what she did to deserve such a wonderful prize, she said that everyone got one! Children are being led to believe that they

are winners and can feel good about themselves just by showing up. Definitely not the way the real world works.

American popular culture exacerbates our self-esteem problem by sending messages to children that they can find success, wealth, and celebrity without any capabilities, effort, or time ("By gosh, I deserve it right now just for being me").[1]

Here is an excerpt from another *Psychology Today* article entitled, "The Gift of Failure":

The self-esteem movement has done an entire generation a deep disservice. It started with the best of intentions. In 1969, Nathaniel Branden wrote a paper entitled "The Psychology of Self-Esteem" that suggested that "feelings of self-esteem were the keys to success in life." Hearing this, many people started to find ways to confer confidence upon our children. This resulted in competitions where everyone gets a trophy, and no one wins. New games attempted to engage children without any winners or losers.

The parents who embraced these efforts did so out of love and with the most noble of intentions. The only problem is that these efforts simply do not work. Self-esteem is not something conferred, it is earned through taking risks and developing skills. When children stretch themselves, they expand their sense of their own capabilities and feel confident to tackle the next challenge. Competence comes from competence—we do not bestow it as a gift.

Relatedly, we also spend too much time protecting our children from any pain or adversity. We hate to see them struggle and we suffer when they suffer. But the same loving envelope that that protects them from pain also protects them from growth.[2]

More and more, schools are removing consequences for most everything, including misbehavior. According to the above excerpt, this is not doing students or society a favor!

Here is material related to the effects of "Every child gets a trophy," In this quotation the "every child gets a trophy" is equivalent to a liberal awarding of "A" grades.

If every child receives a trophy or a medal, it will help them build their self-esteem by protecting them from a perception of failure if they don't receive a trophy . . . right?

UNFORTUNATELY, THIS ALSO IS A MYTH GENERATED BY A MISUNDERSTANDING OF SELF-ESTEEM.

Many parents believe that protecting children from failure will ensure their success through childhood to adulthood. Nothing could be further from the truth. The child that is given the opportunity to fail is the child who is given the opportunity to learn and, ultimately, succeed.

Parents, who focus on the efforts of the child, rather than the outcome or results of their efforts are giving the child freedom to try and if not successful the first time, the desire to try again . . . and again, and again, if necessary!

The most powerful questions a parent can ask their child who has failed are, "Did you give it your best effort? and What could you do differently next time?"

THE PERSON WHO HAS NEVER PERSISTED THROUGH FAILURE TO ACHIEVE SUCCESS HAS LITTLE OR NO CONFIDENCE IN THEIR OWN ABILITY.

This all too often leads to allowing someone else to run their life, and it is rare that anything positive comes from that.

To raise children with strong self-esteem is not to give them trophies for merely "showing up" as this can be detrimental to their self-esteem and eventually their self-confidence and self-efficacy (one's appraisal of oneself of what they can cause, bring about or make happen.)

If a person felt inadequate to face the normal challenges of life, if he or she lacked fundamental self-trust or confidence in his or her mind, we would recognize the presence of a self-esteem deficiency, no matter what other assets the person possessed.[3]

There is quite a lot of literature that says giving grades demotivates and produces bad outcomes. In most cases it is assumed that not using grades unleashes the "mother lode" of intrinsic motivation, the most superior form of motivation. The idea is this; since letter grades are no longer relevant the student will self-actualize into a self-motivated student who will develop a "love of learning" and develop deep understanding in topics of interest.

There is no question this concept will work with some students. Usually, however, this approach works with higher income students and not so good for lower income children. Several colleges offer options to students to use traditional A to F letter grades, selected by course, or to go to a pass/fail scheme. Brown University is one such university.

Here is a case study using materials from this book. In chapter 2, many unfavorable outcomes are listed. Here is an example of "widening the plate": In 1998, 38.9% of high schoolers had an "A" average. By 2016, the rate had increased to 47%. Meanwhile, the average SAT score fell from 1026 to 1002 on the 1600-point scale. If 47% of all high school students have an "A" this means that grading is very similar to a school that has moved away from letter grades.

These easy letter schools are hoping they have unleashed intrinsic motivation in which case student knowledge should have increased. As is shown, SAT scores dropped 24 points over the same period, so the desired motivation did not produce knowledge to improve SAT scores. Look at another chapter 2 reported result:

A national survey shows when parents were asked if their children were performing at or above grade level, 90% said they were. In fact, only 34% were. Here's the research result: According to research[4] from Learning Heroes, "9 out of 10 parents of public-school students, regardless of race, income, and education level, believe their child is at or above grade level in reading and math." However, scores on the 8th grade National Assessment of Educational Progress (NAEP) in 2019, found that barely 34% of students are proficient in both math and reading.[5] Here again no improved motivation and associated knowledge growth.

Lastly, using results from the U.S. National Assessment exams, there has been negligible to zero improvements in reading and math. What has happened to learning? If there was a desire in the public schools to improve motivation it certainly isn't working. Why then do schools "give away" top grades? Here are two reasons:

1. They are attempting to elevate student self-esteem. Based on what was discussed above, this is like everyone gets a trophy. What can anyone say about self-esteem; it can't be measured, but most likely it has declined. The current philosophy certainly hasn't improved learning.
2. By giving unearned "A's," the schools are masking their poor performance thus keeping the heat off them from the parents. After all, the parents say, "My kids are bringing home 'A's'; this school is doing a terrific job." They would be amazed if they looked at international, national, and state test results.

It is not a stretch to look at today's problems with mental diseases and suicides as the by-product of parents who are overprotective and who are unknowingly lowering self-esteem. Let the kids take some risks, let them experience failures, it will build character and develop resilience and the ability to work through setbacks only to come out a better person.

IN SUMMARY

The self-esteem movement began in the early 1970s. Parents and schools went to great lengths to be sure their child's self-esteem was never in jeopardy. There was a major misunderstanding about the correct way to go about maximizing self-esteem. People chose the wrong routes; routes that can lower self-esteem and create a weak basis for building self-confidence, the ideal destination for a child.

Ensuring students do not fail in any aspect of their lives is not the right road. Allow the students to have the opportunity for some small failures so they begin to learn how to deal with a setback. Giving a low performing student an "F" on their paper represents a failure of small proportions. Let the student crank up their resolve and work to never let that happen again. This will condition them for bigger failures that come to all of us as we mature. If they do not improve, at least they are not rewarded for poor work. They will recognize the justice of the receipt of a deserved "F."

NOTES

1. Taylor, Jim, "Popular Culture: America's Self-Esteem Problem Rewarding Children No Matter What They Do Does Not Create Real Self-Esteem," *Psychology Today*, June 7, 2010, https://www.psychologytoday.com/us/blog/the-power-prime/201006/popular-culture-americas-self-esteem-problem

2. Baskin, Steve, "The Gift of Failure, Letting Our Children Struggle Is a Difficult Gift to Give," *Psychology Today*, December 31, 2011, https://www.psychologytoday.com/us/blog/smores-and-more/201112/the-gift-failure

3. Madrid, Jim, "Do Participation Trophies Hurt Self-Esteem?," *Advanced Sports Technologies*, January 2021, https://astacademy.com/f/do-participation-trophies-hurt-self-esteem

4. "Do U.S. Parents Overestimate Their Student's Progress?," *NCEE*, 1/14/21, https://ncee.org/quick-read/do-u-s-parents-overestimate-their-students-progress/

5. "Do U.S. Parents Overestimate Their Student's Progress?," *NCEE*, 1/14/21, https://ncee.org/quick-read/do-u-s-parents-overestimate-their-students-progress/

Chapter 4

Teachers, the Vital Ingredient

Teachers are by far the most important ingredient[1] in the education stew, and by a wide margin. Children can learn in a chicken coop if they have a good teacher. Teachers are important community members and make valuable contributions to society. When George Bernard Shaw wrote in his 1903 play *Man and Superman,* "Those who can, do; those who can't, teach," he probably didn't mean it. These few words have done immensurable harm to teachers over a hundred plus years.

Teachers are intelligent servant leaders who devote their lives to making our children better people. Without teachers, a society will wither and die. Our democracy will fail as citizens turn to despots for their leadership. Most great societies have thrived on universal education, the product of teachers. This quotation speaks to this point:

> Across countries, education and democracy are highly correlated. In our model, schooling teaches people to interact with others and raises the benefits of civic participation, including voting and organizing. In the battle between democracy and dictatorship, democracy has a wide potential base of support but offers weak incentives to its defenders. Dictatorship provides stronger incentives to a narrower base.
>
> As education raises the benefits of civic engagement, it raises participation in support of a broad-based regime (democracy) relative to that in support of a narrow-based regime (dictatorship). This increases the likelihood of successful democratic revolutions against dictatorships and reduces that of successful anti-democratic coups.[2]

Teachers are thrilled when a child finally comes around and says, "Now I see it; thank you for helping me out." If you haven't been a teacher, you are missing one of life's great joys. You are a shepherd, and the children are your flock; you spend each day tending to your flock ensuring each child grows a little under your tutelage. Teachers are thrilled when one of their children accomplishes great things, things they had a hand in. Teachers are to be admired, respected, and loved.

Teachers lead the way to a democracy. In direct opposition to Shaw's quote, this one speaks to teachers.

> Teachers have one of the toughest yet most rewarding jobs out there. It requires a specific calling and a unique set of talents to educate young minds, to keep attention focused and curiosity dialed in. Those who take on the mantle are everyday heroes, from the coach who encourages students to persevere, even when it's tough, to the teacher who goes above and beyond in uncharted waters.
>
> And while it's easy to think of ways teachers have changed our lives, or our children's lives, we can forget that even the most dedicated educators need reminders every now and again that the work they do has meaning and purpose.[3]

One aspect of a teacher's job won't endear them to all students. They measure, they evaluate, and they grade. This aspect of their work usually produces winners and losers unless they hand out all "A's." Teachers understand the setting and enforcement of high standards that is vital for educational excellence.

Without wavering from these preamble paragraphs, it is sad to report that America is turning against many of its teachers, and it is not the teachers' fault. Teachers love to teach but unfortunately, they are being deprived of school environment and the properly reared children that allow them to do their jobs.

WHAT DEFINES A GREAT TEACHER?

Each of us can recall a great teacher. One of the most important skills of a great teacher is that they teach you and you enjoyed it! You may like them as a person, admire their speaking skills, their cleverness, like their ability to explain things clearly and many other attributes. There is one essential outcome, *you learned*. You acquired skills that you believe will serve you well as you mature.

If you learn valuable skills, your feelings about a "mean" teacher will fall by the wayside. It is possible to have a person who wasn't very nice as a teacher or was exceptionally tough but if they made you learn you realize they created value in your life.

At DePauw University there was an accounting professor who gave "pop" exams. Students would show up for class one day and be told to put away their books for a one-hour exam! This demand to always be prepared was an irritation, but it was a wonderful teaching technique. He taught his students, and he taught them well. In later life, his students developed an even keener admiration for Mr. Allen because he "made" them learn skills they needed to be successful.

Learning is the chief result of a great teacher; they added value to your life.

This last sentence about Professor Allen is important. He "made" them learn. This doesn't speak well for those who want to do away with tests and grades. Only a tiny fraction of students will grab hold of the material and master it on their own. They need a shove, they need a hammer, they need incredible desire.

What Are the Attributes of a Great Teacher?

There are many lists like the one quoted below, but this one was selected because of the highly experienced author.

> Years ago, as a young, eager student, I would have told you that a great teacher was someone who provided classroom entertainment and gave very little homework. Needless to say, after many years of K-12 administrative experience and giving hundreds of teacher evaluations, my perspective has changed.
>
> My current position as a professor in higher education gives me the opportunity to share what I have learned with current and future school leaders and allows for some lively discussions among my graduate students in terms of what it means to be a great teacher. I have narrowed down the many characteristics of a great teacher to those I have found to be the most essential, regardless of the age of the learner:
>
> 1. *A great teacher respects students.* In a great teacher's classroom, each person's ideas and opinions are valued. Students feel safe to express their feelings and learn to respect and listen to others. This teacher creates a welcoming learning environment for all students.
> 2. *A great teacher creates a sense of community and belonging in the classroom.* The mutual respect in this teacher's classroom provides a supportive, collaborative environment.
> 3. *A great teacher is warm, accessible, enthusiastic, and caring.* This person is approachable, not only to students, but to everyone on campus. This is the teacher to whom students know they can go with any problems or concerns or even to share a funny story. Great teachers possess good listening skills and take time out of their way-too-busy schedules for anyone who needs them.
> 4. *A great teacher sets high expectations for all students.* This teacher realizes that the expectations she has for her students greatly affect their achievement; she knows that students *generally give to teachers as much or as little as is expected of them.*[4]
> 5. *A great teacher has his own love of learning* and inspires students with his passion for education and for the course material.

6. *A great teacher is a skilled leader.* Different from administrative leaders, effective teachers focus on shared decision making and teamwork, as well as on community building.
7. *A great teacher can "shift gears"* and is flexible when a lesson isn't working. This teacher assesses his teaching throughout the lessons and finds new ways to present material to make sure that every student understands the key concepts.
8. *A great teacher collaborates with colleagues on an ongoing basis.* Rather than thinking of herself as weak because she asks for suggestions or help, this teacher views collaboration as a way to learn from a fellow professional. A great teacher uses constructive criticism and advice as an opportunity to grow as an educator.
9. *A great teacher maintains professionalism in all areas*—from personal appearance to organizational skills and preparedness for each day. Her communication skills are exemplary, whether she is speaking with an administrator, one of her students or a colleague.[5]

How Do You Make a Teacher Great?

Here are comments from Bill Gates. When Mr. Gates uses the term "we" he is referring to the Bill and Melinda Gates Foundation. They have spent millions working to improve U.S. education.

How Do Great Teachers Make a Difference?

We have funded scholarships. We've done things in libraries. A lot of these things had a good effect. But the more we looked at it, the more we realized that having great teachers was the very key thing. So, we hooked up with some people studying how much variation is there between teachers, between say, the top quartile (the very best) and the bottom quartile. How much variation is there within a school or between schools? And the answer is that these variations are absolutely unbelievable.

A top quartile teacher will increase the performance of their class based on test scores by over 10% in a single year. What does that mean? Well, it means that if the entire U.S. had top quartile teachers for two years, the entire difference between U.S. and Asia would go away and within four years we would be blowing everyone in the world away. So, it's simple: All you need is those top quartile teachers. So, you'd say well wow, that's good. We should reward those people and we should retain those people.

We should find out what they're doing and transfer that skill to other people. But I can tell you that absolutely is not happening today. What are the characteristics of this top quartile? What do they look like? You might think, well, these must be very senior teachers, and the answer is no. *Once somebody is taught for three years, their teaching quality does not change thereafter. The variation is very small.*

You might think well, these are people with master's degrees. They've gone back, and they've gotten their Master of Education. This chart *[see video for chart]* takes four different factors and says how much do they explain teaching quality. That bottom thing, which says there's no effect at all, that's a master's degree. Now, the way the pay system works is there are two things that are rewarded: one is seniority because your pay goes up and you vest in your pension, and the second is giving extra money to people who get their master's degree, but it is in no way associated with being a better teacher.

Teach for America has a slight effect. Math teachers majoring in math has a measurable effect, but overwhelmingly it's your past performance. There are some people who are very good at this, and we've done almost nothing to study what that is and how to draw it out in order to replicate it. To raise the average capability and to encourage the people with it to stay in the system.

You might say, Will the good teachers stay and the bad teachers leave? The answer is, on average, the slightly better teachers leave the system and it's a system with very high turnover.[6]

How to Make Existing Teachers Better

Here is a Japanese word you may not know, *kaizen*. Kaizen is a compound of two Japanese words that together translate as "good change" or "improvement." However, kaizen has come to mean "continuous improvement" through its association with lean manufacturing methodology and principles. Kaizen has its origins in post-World War II Japanese quality circles. In a kaizen-based organization there is constant attention paid to "getting better each day." Its contribution to improving business operations is huge. It works because everyone pitches in to improve operations by making many small changes, something that everyone can do.

So, How Can It Be Applied in a School?

The State of Maryland (to be discussed in chapter 14) is embarking on a major renovation of their education system. In response to a common teacher complaint, there is no career path for teachers, they have created such a path. Table 4.1 shows the four levels on the teacher career path.

A single "Professor Master Teacher" is needed per school. This teacher should focus on quality control and kaizen. To be sure, they are the lead teacher for the entire school, and they have authority to work anywhere that needs them. The professor master teachers are like a team captain of the teaching team. Their relationship with the teacher is as a peer, someone who will work with them to make the school better.

Table 4.1. Teacher Career Path

Teacher Career Path	
Title	**Expected Teaching Time per Day**
Teacher	60%
Lead Teacher	50%
Master Teacher	40%
Professor Master Teacher	20%

Here's an example. The fifth-grade teachers are not happy with the way they are teaching basic math and they ask the lead teacher to listen to one of their math lessons. The professor master teacher convenes an after-school session with all the fifth-grade teachers. She leads them through the analysis of what they have been doing and works with them to find better ways to deliver the material. After this discussion the lead teacher outlines what they have agreed to do and gives them a copy for tomorrow's lesson. Spelling may be the topic tomorrow. Their collective approach will help them to improve. This is how the lead teacher spends their time.

The lead teacher also visits the classes looking for improvements of all kinds and works with the teacher to implement the improvements. This must be a collegial relationship for it to work properly. If they become a judge, the teachers will not trust them. Another way this person can help is with classroom management, a major challenge for most teachers. They should be experts on classroom management because it is an issue in almost all schools. This kind of coaching activity puts the school on a continuous improvement path, a path that will produce significant positive changes.

ARE TEACHERS HAPPY?

Are teachers happy? No, they are very unhappy. The common assumption says they are unhappy because they are underpaid. This may be true but that is not the primary reason. They are unhappy because of working conditions. While in the classroom, they must endure lack of respect, profane names, lost teaching time from disruptive students, and ofttimes poor school management. To illustrate: A principal told his teacher, if there is ever a disagreement or problem between you and a child, "I will stand up for the child."

Does the management "have the teachers' backs"? In his case the answer is no! Why would a principal throw his teacher under the train so readily? The answer comes in chapter 12; they are deathly afraid of being sued by a parent. This is a major black mark on the teacher and expensive proposition for a cash strapped school. The threat of suit has warped everything in the schools.

Current teachers do not have much to say about their children's behavior, after all it is part of their responsibility to control their children. Retired teachers will deliver an earful of reality. They say the children are terrible and most do not care about learning. They want to spend time on their cell phones and don't want to be bothered with school. Retired teachers also have bad things to say about parents; they are the reason the children are so disrespectful.

Recently a relative quit her teaching job for several reasons, one of which was a lack of respect. She was tired of being called "bitch" and other terribly disrespectful terms. If you as a reader have doubts about the seemingly extreme nature of these words, go to the website elevateteachers.org, click on Lessons and then view Lesson 4. It is the story of a top teacher resigning from the Green Bay, Wisconsin, school system. The teacher reports her concerns to the entire school board in a public session and her concerns are awful! She tells about the crude and vulgar things teachers are being called and the chaos and danger for the staff as well as the children.

An *Education Week* article speaks to the topic of teacher satisfaction.

> Teachers' job satisfaction levels appear to have hit an all-time low this year as the fallout from the COVID-19 pandemic continues to ravage schools. That's according to the Merrimack College Teacher Survey, a nationally representative poll of more than 1,300 teachers conducted by the Ed Week Research Center and commissioned by the Winston School of Education and Social Policy at Merrimack College.[7]

The survey, which was conducted between January 9 and February 23, 2023, was designed to replace the MetLife Survey of the American Teacher, which ran for more than 25 years and ended in 2012. Figure 4.1 shows the latest result.

The solid line begins in about 1983 and ends in 2012 when the Metropolitan Life Insurance Company stopped surveying teachers. Their portion of the graph shows a precipitous drop beginning around 2008 and continuing down when they stopped the survey in 2011. The Merrimack College data was collected in 2022 and reported in 2023. It is a national sample from over 1,300 teachers. There is a 10-year gap that can only be imagined as a continuation of the Met Life work.

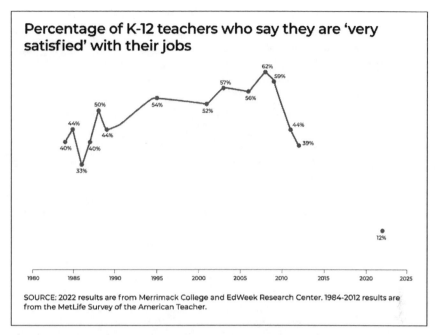

Percentage of K-12 teachers who say they are 'very satisfied' with their jobs

SOURCE: 2022 results are from Merrimack College and EdWeek Research Center. 1984-2012 results are from the MetLife Survey of the American Teacher.

Figure 4.1. Percentage of K-12 Teachers Who Say They Are "Very Satisfied" with Their Jobs

Look carefully to see the last data point in the lower right-hand portion of the graph; it's way down there by itself. The point indicates only 12% of the responding teachers claimed they were very satisfied with their jobs. The response to this question peaked in 2008 at 62%. That's a huge decline.

Here's supporting commentary from the same article:

The results paint a picture of a disillusioned, exhausted workforce. A little more than half of teachers are satisfied with their jobs, and only 12% say they're "very satisfied" with their jobs, down from 39% in 2012. More than half of teachers said they likely wouldn't advise their younger self to pursue a career in teaching.

What teachers want is to be able to teach and teach well, and if they can't do it because their students are unmanageable, because they have a toxic work environment, that discourages them from acting as teachers who are learning and growing and getting better and increasing their commitment to the work, said Susan Moore Johnson, a Harvard University professor of education who studies teachers' working conditions and satisfaction. That's the side of satisfaction we need to pay attention to—it's not just keeping people in their positions.

The survey found that about a quarter of teachers don't feel like students' parents or guardians respect them. In interviews, teachers said some parents can be combative and demanding, with little regard for their professional expertise.[8]

Clearly, this shows a large number of teachers are not happy in their work. It all boils down to this: They went into teaching with a strong desire to change student lives for the better, but for them, it isn't happening. They are not able to do their jobs and they will not be happy until they can.

TEACHER SUPPLY AND DEMAND

Education institutions at all levels are having trouble hiring teachers, teacher aids, and so forth, and it is getting worse. As this discussion concludes, teachers are not happy. They have many complaints, salary being only one of them. Because of this, they are discouraging others from going into teaching. How do these negative attitudes affect teacher supply? What does research uncover to better define this problem?

A 2016 report from the Learning Policy Institutes offers a good analysis of the supply/demand problem. Here is their introductory paragraph:

> Widespread media reports of local teacher shortages have become a hot topic in education since the summer of 2015. After years of teacher layoffs, districts began hiring again as the economy recovered from the Great Recession. Many were surprised to find they had serious difficulty finding qualified teachers for their positions, especially in fields like mathematics, science, special education, and bilingual education/English language development.
>
> Several states greatly expanded emergency permits to allow hiring of untrained teachers to meet these demands, which is the classic definition of a shortage. To date, however, there has not yet been a detailed national analysis of the sources and extent of these shortages, or a prognosis for the future.[9]

Figure 4.2 shows the future supply and demand.[10] This chart shows the bottom falling out on supply. The difference between supply and demand for 2025 is 200,000 teachers with a total output of teachers at 115,000. The difference for 2022 is 159,000. Looking at this last number, it seems too large; if the shortfall was really this big there would be more pressure in the system. Is there any way to check this total shortfall from another source? Yes, here is a look at the shortfall from *Education Week*.

> The researchers estimate that there are more than 36,500 teacher vacancies in the nation. They also estimate that there are more than 163,500 positions filled by teachers who aren't fully certified or are not certified in the subject area they're teaching.[11]

Test the shortfall predicted by figure 4.2. It predicts a shortage of 159,000 in 2022. Is this realistic, is there tremendous pressure in the system? Actually

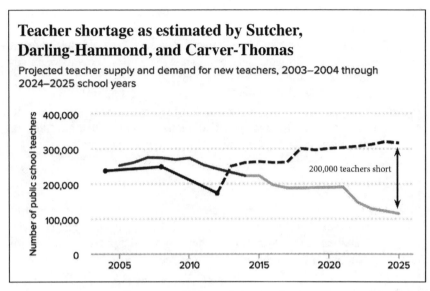

Teacher shortage as estimated by Sutcher, Darling-Hammond, and Carver-Thomas

Projected teacher supply and demand for new teachers, 2003–2004 through 2024–2025 school years

Figure 4.2. Teacher Shortage as Estimated by Sutcher, Darling-Hammond, and Carver-Thomas

no. With 163,500 positions that are filled using emergency teaching certificates there is much less pressure. Pressure will grow if these new hires cannot teach and simply babysit. On the other hand, if these "off the street" hires are successful it's a new ball game. It opens the door wide for new hires.

What about teacher production? The production of teachers in 2005 was around 252,000; the production in 2025 is projected to be 114,900. In 2005 the system could produce 252,000 teachers so at only 114,900 it is then only running at 45% of its 2005 capacity. Is this plausible?

Based on what is happening around the country in schools of education, it seems very plausible.

So, there is a major train wreck that has already started. Suppose all the stops are pulled and a huge effort is put forward to reverse the massive drop in students majoring in education. Restoring this teacher shortfall is going to take years. One of the most important and most difficult steps is to make the classroom a pleasant place for teachers and a place where they can do their job, teach. Even people hired on emergency certificates will expect to be respected and will not work in a lion's den.

To reverse the classroom environment means discipline and respect can no longer be an issue and teachers can spend their precious 220 minutes teaching. Chapter 6 will consider some fairly drastic measures to work in this direction. This will be a major problem because one of the root causes of the disruptive behavior for the younger children is poor parenting, which is difficult to fix.

If the student begins school at 3 years old there is an opportunity to teach good behavior habits. Suppose this is the case, it will take many years for these students to work their way into the upper grades. Next comes pay; pay must be increased. This is the topic for the next subsection of this book.

Lastly comes the university education and the appeal made to students to go into education. This will probably add another 8 years. Overall, this is a 15- to 18-year journey unless very drastic measures are put into place.

How Much Money Should a Teacher Be Paid?

The answer to this question is very simple: *whatever it takes to draw them out of the general labor pool into the classrooms*. The state of Maryland believes this number is about $80,000 per year. They studied the pay of jobs that are filled by folks with a four-year university degree and decided that was their competition for labor. Work in education no longer has a unique hold on people, especially women.

Women, in particular, used to be drawn to teaching because it was a calling and likely one they would follow into a lifelong career. In all candor, in years gone by, they did not have a lot of other opportunities. This is no longer the case; they have a whole new world of opportunity. They can do almost anything they choose. Don't believe for a minute that more pay is all it takes. People see the evening news where life in the classroom is portrayed as dangerous and chaotic. No amount of money is going to motivate anyone to step into a chaotic and dangerous classroom.

In summary, America is in trouble, in trouble because parents are not doing a proper job of rearing their children. In trouble because these children's actions and disrespect for teachers is destroying the system. For some teachers, the parents can be as big of a problem as their children. Solving this problem is not going to be easy but having the willingness to remove disruptive children from regular classes and to expel the worst of the worst will go a long way toward a much-improved system.

NOTES

1. This chapter is about public-school and charter schoolteachers. What is reported does not apply to religious or private schools. For the most part teachers there are pleased with their jobs and have a different and more easily managed collection of children.

2. Glaser, Edward, Ponzetto, Giacomo A., Shleifer, Andrei, "Why Does Democracy Need Education? *Harvard Scholar*, May 31, 2007, published online, https://scholar .harvard.edu/files/shleifer/files/democracy_final_jeg.pdf

3. Hall, Leah, "23 A+ Education Quotations for Teachers to Inspire Their Passion," *Country Living*, July 28, 2022, https://www.countryliving.com/life/ g40684352/inspiring-educational-quotes-for-teachers/?utm_source=google&utm _medium=cpc&utm_campaign=arb_ga_clv_md_pmx_us_urlx_18605327224&gclid =EAIaIQobChMImKHvv9fq_QIVNmpvBB2g2gWqEAAYASAAEgKzK_D_BwE

4. Author's note. Here is why high standards must be created. If not much is expected, that is exactly what you will get.

5. Orlando, Mara EdD, "Nine Characteristics of a Great Teacher," *Faculty Focus*, Jan. 4, 2013, https://www.facultyfocus.com/articles/philosophy-of-teaching/nine -characteristics-of-a-great-teacher/

6. Gates, Bill, "How Do You Make a Teacher Great, Part 1," taken from a transcription of this Ted talk, https://www.youtube.com/watch?v=OnfzZEREfQs

7. Will, Madeline, "Teacher Satisfaction Hits an All Time Low," *Education Week*, April 14, 2022, https://www.edweek.org/teaching-learning/teacher-job-satisfaction -hits-an-all-time-low/2022/04

8. Ibid.

9. Sutcher, Leib, Darling-Hammond, Linda, "A Coming Crisis in Teaching, Teacher Supply, Demand, and Shortages in the U.S.," *The Learning Institute*, September 2016.

10. Garcia, Emma, Weiss, Elaine, "The teacher shortage is real, large, and growing, and worse than we thought the first report in 'The Perfect Storm in the Teacher Labor Market' series," *Economic Policy Institute*, March 26, 2019, https://files.epi.org/pdf /163651.pdf

11. Will, Madeline, "How Bad Is the Teacher Shortage? What Two New Studies Say," *Education Week*, Sept 6, 2022, https://www.edweek.org/leadership/how-bad-is -the-teacher-shortage-what-two-new-studies-say/2022/09

Chapter 5

220 Precious Minutes

This chapter will illustrate how the precious daily 220 minutes of instructional time is calculated and how it is eroded due to "lost time events." These minutes are where the "rubber meets the road" in education. Lose this time and learning suffers; lose large quantities of this time and learning is nearly impossible.

Most state laws mandate a certain number of at-school days per school year; in Indiana this number is 180 days.

Table 5.1 illustrates how a typical 420-minute (7 hour) school day is utilized.

Of the full school day, 220 minutes or 52% of the day is dedicated to formal classroom instruction under the same teacher. There is a 60 minute out of class instruction period for art, gym, and so forth. Since that is another teacher, it is not counted in the 220 minutes.

Considering a full 180-day school calendar, a student spends 1,260 hours, or 14% of a year, at school. Of this, 660 hours is instructional time; this is 8% of a student's life for one year, assuming they go to class.

Many people feel the schools should play a bigger role in shaping the child's character but, with only a 14% exposure to the children, the school doesn't have much chance to influence them.

PRECIOUS TIME

Consider yourself in that classroom and you have a big agenda, as described in your lesson plan, to fulfill each day. Your task is to bring the children forward daily in a planful way to meet the requirements of the curriculum. You have just begun your teaching when one of your students has a fit, screaming and throwing anything at hand and refuses to settle down.

No matter what they do you cannot touch them because doing so may get you and the school sued. You do your best to "talk them down" and finally

Table 5.1. School Instructional Time for a Typical Day/7 hours per day

School Instructional Time for a Typical Day - 7 hours per day		Minutes per Day	Percent of Day
Total time Kids are at School		420	100%
Less:	Lunch/Recess	75	
	Class start-up & shut down	45	
	Out of Class Instruction	60	
	Rest Room Breaks	20	
Classroom Instructional Time		220	52%

they take a seat, and you begin where you left off. However, you now have 23 fewer minutes, as well as a room full of disturbed children, to complete your busy agenda. This rather large disturbance might happen again but most likely there will be several smaller ones, but you must work around these events and carry on.

The reality of the matter is that when this day becomes an everyday pattern, you do not have enough time to meet the school's teaching goals. The entire classroom suffers due to the actions of a small group of children. The kids are not keeping up, they are not learning nearly enough.

Who is at fault here? Is it the teacher or the student? It's the teacher who has the responsibility to manage the class, to fully engage the students so they want to pay attention and learn. Most teacher preparation programs do not provide training that will improve the odds that the teacher will be better equipped to take control.

What about the children? The next chapter looks at and measures the negative impact that children's unruly behavior has on the class.

The teachers in the study (discussed in chapter 6) were all experienced, and they admitted that the disruptive children were so out of control they could not manage them. Can this be an acceptable excuse? Indeed, many of today's children are unusually rude and disrespectful. Who's to blame for this? The answer is not one that folks want to hear but most already know what it is, it's the parents. Poor parenting is the root cause of many of today's poorly behaved children The reason this conclusion is not welcomed is that it will not be easy to fix. More on this in chapter 6.

Formalizing this thinking process, consider the events that occur before a school suspends a student. This material is taken from the book, *The Kids Are Smart Enough, So What's the Problem?*[1] Nobody wants to suspend a student, but something must be done to try to change their behavior and to stop their wasting so much precious instructional time.

The Anatomy of a Suspension

This discussion will carry the loss of time a step further. Why do schools suspend students? This loss of time is only one of the reasons for a suspension: other reasons are hostile behavior, bullying another student, or fighting.

The local public radio station recently featured a discussion about a young man who had been suspended from school. The host was interviewing a social worker whose job it was to work with the young man to prepare him to return to school. The tone of the discussion was one that supposed a school/teacher failure for the student's suspension. Great effort was expended to blame everyone but the young man.

To better understand how this suspension looks from a teacher's point of view, a deeper study will be made of a typical suspension case. This discussion is positioned around a student who is ultimately suspended to better explain how their behavior can diminish teacher effectiveness. Not only will this case study be helpful to explain the behavior of a *disruptive* student, but it will also further illustrate how lost instruction time is created as the teacher deals with the various events.

This fabricated timeline shows that the offending student has had a series of issues in the classroom over the days before the suspension. This is not an actual case, but it is a series of plausible disruptions that would be likely with a *disruptive* student.

To better understand how this suspension looks from a teacher's point of view and from the perspective of lost instructional time, consider the timeline presented in figure 5.1.

In these four days with the student, the teacher should have had 880 minutes of instruction time, but this single (there may be others as well) child wasted 111 minutes or 12.6%. In addition to the students not learning, it is demoralizing to the teacher.

The teacher and administration believe action must be taken to send this child a message. They cannot tolerate this behavior; something must change. They call the parents and tell them not to send him to school for 5 days. That this will "shape them up" is not likely but it will give the teacher relief from the student's disruptive behavior.

This probably punishes the parents more than the child but hopefully their time spent home with the child can be put to good use and they work to correct the problem.

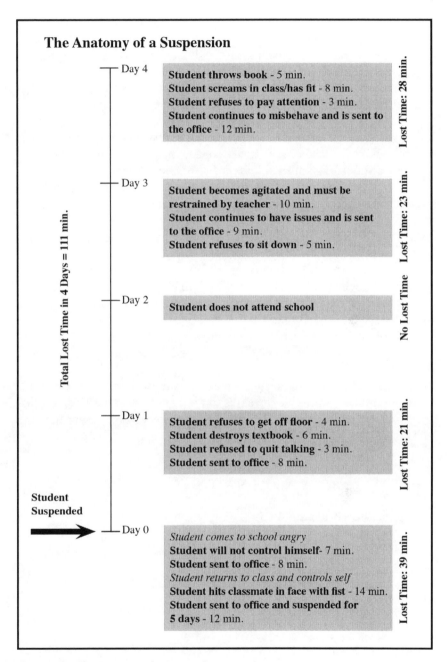

Figure 5.1. The Anatomy of a Suspension

Another case presents a different scenario: An intellectually disabled child is placed in the classroom with the understanding that they won't learn much, but something is better than nothing. They disrupt the class with their behavior, but it is not malicious. Is it right for this student to be in the class? It turns the teacher into a babysitter, it steals time from the other 24 kids, and the overall benefit to the special child is minimal. In the eyes of this businessman, the child should be removed from the class and placed in a class that provides a more managed environment. The other children have priority on the teacher's time, and they need every minute to make their forward progression.

America suffers monumental losses of instruction due to misbehaving students. There is ample public knowledge of these events, and this knowledge is driving teachers away from classroom jobs. What person wants to walk into the lion's den of a classroom and subject themselves to this kind of environment? If not fixed, it will lead to even more potential teachers opting to select another career.

This chapter explains the very commonsense outcomes that occur when the children are not controllable. This is one of the bigger reasons America's test scores are not acceptable; the teachers do not get the time they need to give proper instruction. This is one of the big reasons that schools of education are running well below their capacity; teaching is not a good path. A principal of a major Indianapolis high school says she would never recommend a student go into teaching!

This description of lost teaching time events must be put in perspective. There are teachers who have the skills to properly control their classrooms. They are few and far between. They possess the needed skills to generate the kind of love and respect all the students need.

NOTE

1. Op. cit., Garrett, Richard W., p 53.

Chapter 6

Discipline Issues Are
a Major Problem

It is not allowed that one student will destroy the learning time of another student.

This statement is the guiding light for this chapter. The focus will be on the children who come to school to learn and who are being deprived of instruction time by disruptive children.

In the United States, much attention is paid to the children who are "acting up" but little or no attention is paid to the other students in the class. The TV shows a news video of a child who needs to be removed from class because of her loud outbursts. She will not let go of her chair, so a policeman tries to wedge her loose and she is tossed around a bit, nothing serious. How much time did this episode take? First the teacher tried to act, but the rules do not allow her to touch the child; the child ignores the teacher's verbal pleas.

Next, the teacher calls for the policeman to come and help; the policeman tries to "talk her down" but she will not let go. Next, mild force is applied but the girl is strong and will not comply. Finally, the policeman applies more force, but she still hangs on. The last scene shows the student on the floor still clutching her chair. In this example, the policeman was fired for his stern actions; under the circumstances a grave injustice to him.

He is trying to preserve teaching time and sometimes that requires drastic actions. Less drastic actions were tried but didn't work. How long do we want this disruption to last? Folks would change their minds about such things if they attended classes to see how chaotic conditions can get.

How many precious minutes did this episode take? The minutes we are interested in are defined as follows: Time loss begins when the teacher's actions to quiet down the student begins and ends, not when the girl and the policeman leave, but later after the class settles down and learning begins again. This disruption could have easily cost 40 minutes. That is 18% of the instruction day that has been lost to all students and will most likely never be made up. Students can't afford to lose so much time and still be expected to do well on knowledge exams.

This event also ruined the day for the teacher as she asks herself, "Why do I have to put up with such disruptions; I can't do my job." All teachers want is to be able to do their jobs, to change children's lives. That's why they chose teaching.

This example also illustrates why teachers refuse to be held accountable for test results. There are many factors beyond their control that effect the test results. They cannot remove the offending children from the room and kids are too undisciplined for the teacher to be able to effectively manage.

DISCIPLINE AND RESPECT ARE HUGE PROBLEMS IN OUR PUBLIC SCHOOLS

The website, elevateteachers.org,[1] set up a small teacher-based study titled, "What's it Like to Teach in a School Graded D?" The teachers on the study team reinforce that student behaviors in the classroom are very distressing and terrible wasteful. One of the major focus points of this study team was to quantify the amount of teaching time lost in each classroom each day due to disruptive children. This information will help to explain to the public why teachers are so distressed and frustrated. The results of this study are presented later in this chapter and help to explain why learning is reduced and why teaching is so unpopular.

The Importance of Classroom Management

Effective classroom management is a prerequisite to an effective learning environment. Children can't learn when they are distracted by inappropriate behavior. A well-managed classroom thus allows meaningful teaching and learning to take place.

The descriptor "meaningful" is important in the above statement. It highlights another reason classroom management is so important. Saying that children learn nothing in a poorly managed classroom is not accurate. In a poorly managed classroom, children do learn. However, they learn the wrong lessons.

In a poorly managed classroom, children learn that serious engagement with serious subjects is not valued. They learn that self-discipline and hard work aren't necessary. In short, poor classroom management stunts children's social-emotional development.

When they don't face consequences, children don't learn to regulate their own behavior. When children see their teacher's attention drained by classmates' misbehavior, they learn that their own needs don't matter.

Effective classroom management, thus, ensures that children learn the right lessons. These lessons are important components of a child's academic, social, and emotional development.

Furthermore, effective behavior management in the classroom promotes student engagement. A well-managed classroom allows all students to participate fully in the learning environment.[2]

Read this article very carefully. It makes some very important points; points that will be emphasized in this book.

1. Students learn the wrong lessons in a poorly managed classroom.
2. They learn serious engagement with serious subjects is not valued.
3. They learn that self-discipline and hard work aren't necessary.
4. Poor classroom management stunts a child's social-emotional development.
5. When they don't face consequences, children don't learn to regulate their own behavior.
6. Effective classroom management, thus, ensures that children learn the right lessons.

Aren't these important skills for all children to learn? To not act and correct these issues is to lose these important skills in all our children. We must have well-managed classrooms!

Here's another revealing story.

I receive a steady stream of missives from teachers, ex-teachers, and other folks who have insider knowledge of America's schools. They all say the same thing, classroom discipline is falling apart and has been for some time, and ask the same question: What can be done?

Public-school administrators, not all, but entirely too many, refuse to acknowledge the problem. When I bring the subject up, they dismiss it, as in, "Oh, it's not as bad as people make it out to be" whereas every teacher I've spoken to in the past twenty years has told me it's worse than the public even imagines and getting worse with every passing year.

One insider recently wrote: "Excellent teachers are giving up. They send kids to the office when they're disruptive, and in minutes the child is back after having received a cookie or some other treat while they talked about their 'feelings.' Also, almost every teacher says that when they call a parent about a child's behavior, the parent makes excuses or blames the teacher."

That description is typical. I will simply add that not only are many good teachers leaving, but many good students are as well. They are either moving to private schools (where a disproportionate number of public-school teachers send their kids) or being home-schooled. As a result of this exodus, the per capita rate of problem students rises. Add in the steady increase in under-disciplined children coming to kindergarten and the question becomes: What will public education look like in ten years if these trends continue?

They are, with rare exception, dedicated people. Teachers are not the problem, not for the most part at least. The problem consists of equal parts irresponsible parenting (not confined to any given demographic), parents who make excuses for brats they send to school (just another form of irresponsible parenting), teacher unions that have been given legal power to game the system, federal aid to education (long outlived its usefulness), and administrators who strip teachers of permission to discipline and then discipline teachers who have the temerity to do so.[3]

Articles like this are replete on the web. This article paints a realistic picture of what is happening in our schools, including the denials by school administrators.

HOW BIG IS THE DISCIPLINE PROBLEM?[4]

After much research looking for studies that assess lost time due to discipline issues, nothing even close has been uncovered. In addition, a professional expert on education is also unaware of any similar project; this expert was engaged to assist in the early phases of this project. A related report's results were obtained by a different process. It found similar results regarding misbehaving children by using surveys; consequently, it had no quantification of percentage of disruptive students and lost classroom time.

In May 2004 the Brooklyn think tank, Public Agenda, published a report entitled: *Teaching Interrupted: Do Discipline Policies in Today's Public Schools Foster the Common Good?*[5] Here is material from their website to tell us who they are.

> *Public Agenda is a nonprofit, nonpartisan organization that helps diverse leaders and citizens navigate divisive, complex issues and work together to find solutions.*
>
> Through nonpartisan research and public engagement, we provide the insights, tools and support people needed to build common ground and arrive at solutions that work for them. In doing so, we are proving that it is possible to make progress on critical issues regardless of our differences.

They say, in all their work, they seek to help build a democracy in which problem solving triumphs over gridlock and inertia, and where public policy reflects the thoughtful input and values of the nation's citizens. Public Agenda was founded in 1975 by social scientist and author Daniel Yankelevich, and former Secretary of State Cyrus Vance. They work to help leaders and citizens move toward solutions on a variety of issues.

Their study relied on a national random sample of 725 middle and high school teachers and 600 parents of middle and high school students. The surveys provide a detailed look at the discipline issue, looking for its causes, the effectiveness of current policies, and the impact on school climate and receptivity to various solutions.

Information From Public Agenda's Executive Summary

These findings confirm that research previously discussed illustrates a problem that exists throughout the nation: Many of their results are presented since this study is so relevant to this book and because their findings are so important.

The vast majority of both teachers (85%) and parents (73%) say that the school experience of most students suffers at the expense of a few chronic offenders.

Most teachers (78%) report that students who are persistent behavior problems should be removed from the school grounds but are not removed.

Too many students are losing critical opportunities for learning—and too many teachers are leaving the profession because of a few persistent troublemakers. What's more, say teachers, today's misbehaving students are quick to remind them that students have rights, and their parents can sue.[6]

Here are some of the additional study conclusions that are relevant to this book:

Nearly half (49%) of the teachers complain they have been accused of unfairly disciplining a student.

More than half (55%) say that districts backing down from assertive parents causes discipline problems.

It's almost unanimously accepted among teachers (98%) that a school needs good discipline and behavior to flourish, and 78% of parents agree.

It is also widely accepted among both groups that part of a school's mission— in addition to teaching the three R's—is to teach kids to follow the rules so they can become productive citizens (teachers 93% and parents 88%).

Students pay a heavy price academically when schools tolerate the chronic bad behavior of the few. Most teachers (77%) admit their teaching would be a lot more effective if they didn't have to spend so much time dealing with disruptive students.[7]

Look at some of the report's root causes for the problems in today's schools.

Topping the list of causes of behavior problems in the nation's schools is parents' failure to teach their children discipline (teachers 82% and parents 74%).

Second on the list is: There's disrespect everywhere in our culture—students absorb it and bring it to school (73% and 68%).[8]

Dealing with persistent troublemakers:

Seventy percent of teachers and 68% of parents strongly support the establishment of "zero tolerance" policies so students know they will be kicked out of school for various violations, with another 23% of teachers and 20% of parents indicating they support this idea somewhat (Total support 93% teachers and 89% parents).

In addition, 46% of teachers and 33% of parents strongly support giving principals a lot more authority to handle discipline issues as they see fit, with another 33% of teachers and 73% of parents supporting this idea somewhat (Total support: 84% teachers; 74% parents).[9]

Putting more responsibility on parents:

A strong majority of teachers (69%) say finding ways to hold parents more accountable for kids' behavior would be a very effective solution to the schools' discipline problems.[10]

Comments on Public Agenda's Report

This report goes further than the school project research (to be discussed below) in that it includes the issue of lawsuits. The teachers never mentioned a fear of being sued in all the team's discussions. Otherwise, it too reports, just as has been explained in this book, that a percentage of troublemakers are costing classroom time and causing teachers to leave the profession.

What is surprising is the high percentage of the parents who know about these issues. This report was released in May 2004, and it does not seem as though it had much impact. Hours and hours of research focused on misbehaving students and lost classroom time never uncovered a single reference to *Teaching Interrupted*. Luckily it was discovered because it establishes the national scope of the classroom problem.

Here again, the absolute reluctance of professional educators to, in any way, associate themselves with work blaming students (really parents) for the problems in many classrooms. In the current environment, to do this "one off" would probably cost them their jobs. The public just does not want to hear this argument; in their eyes, it's the teacher's job to manage the classroom. Generally, this would not be an unreasonable expectation but in today's world, a fairly high percentage of the children around the country are not manageable by most teachers.

Given the current trends, these problems will not be resolved before there is a major crisis in the teaching profession brought about by the fact that too few young people want to devote their lives to teaching. This trend has already started and is well on its way.

How Many Schools?

Based on this work from Public Agenda, how many U.S. public schools have problems with classroom discipline? The U.S. has about 100,000 public schools; from the report, about 80% of these schools have lost instruction minutes. Putting these two together gives:

80,00 Public Schools Have Lost Instructional
Time Due to Disruptive Children.

Now that there is some sense the size of the discipline problem, the next question is how to determine the level of lost classroom time. This method will be discussed below.

Estimating Lost Instruction Time

In 2013, a small study team was formed at a Marion County, Indiana, elementary school to determine why their school earned a "D" grade in the first official Indiana school grading exercise. Team members spent much of their time examining the makeup of their classes and measuring the amount of time wasted by disruptive students.

As best judged by the absence of these ideas in the literature, this exercise is original work. Though it is primitive, it is hoped that high-powered university researchers will expand this kind of measurement approach and make it even better. Knowledge about the size of classroom losses will be valuable in establishing discipline policy.

ALL STUDENTS CAN BE POSITIONED
ON A BEHAVIORAL SPECTRUM

Teachers say that the makeup of their classes (they add, any class) can be described by placing each student on a spectrum of student types. As would be expected, there are good students and bad, there are students who listen to instructions and do their work and there are others who are not so good. As this discussion unfolded this spectrum was established:

> *The Engaged Student*..................*The Followers*
> ....*The Disruptive Student*

The teachers are very concerned about a proportion of their students (the *disruptives*) who are so difficult to manage; those students who dramatically affect the learning process of the entire classroom.

While students seldom clearly fall into a clear category on the spectrum, and their position can vary over time, these three categories are going to simplify the discussion. Here are the teachers' definitions of these three student types.

The Engaged Student

Engaged students can be counted on to act with integrity most of the time. They are the ones who stay in their seats and keep working quietly if the teacher must step out of the room. When their teacher is teaching, their eyes are either on the teacher, or on the material that is being taught. Either way, they are actively listening and participating in the lesson. When given an assignment, they get busy immediately. They will sit at their desk or in their assigned spot and work. They raise their hand if they have trouble.

Regardless the circumstances, they are actively listening and participating in the lesson. Because these students are self-motivated learners, it's rare that they do not get their work done. They follow procedures, accept consequences without attitude, and are always honest with the teacher. Engaged students are often the most academically successful students. Should teachers ever need to call home, which is rare, the parents are supportive, and the issue is handled.

The Followers

Followers are the most complex category and ar often the most common type of student. They are heavily influenced by the students around them. When a *follower* is around a group of *engaged* students, the *follower* will behave like an *engaged* student. More often, however, when the *follower* is around a *disruptive* student, then they will behave like the *disruptive* student. Academically, *follower* students vary across the intellectual spectrum and follow a typical student talent distribution curve.

Most *follower* students will get their homework and class work completed. However, if a *follower* is working with a *disruptive*, the assignment tends not to get completed. A *follower* is generally more willing to accept the consequences of their choices, but some *followers* will deny that they did anything wrong. A phone call home will generally receive a positive response from a parent; however, the behavior is less likely to be resolved. It may stop for a few days, but it will eventually reappear.

The Disruptive Students

Disruptive students are the ones who rarely make good choices in the classroom. They cannot be trusted to make good decisions when left alone. They rarely do their homework, and getting them to complete class work is very difficult, often requiring the teacher to stand near the student. These students do not take responsibility for their actions, and blame others for their choices. When corrected, these students can become belligerent, attitudinal, or act as if they don't care.

These students are frequently bullies and will not hesitate to initiate conflict against their peers and sometimes against their teachers. Many are also highly subversive, not out-and-out causing conflict, but often creating conflict by spreading rumors or instigating others to fight. A phone call home does not solve the problem. These parents have gotten phone calls from their child's teachers for years about the same problems.

The sad reality is that many parents of these students have as many issues as the student and can become confrontational with the teacher. Some tell the teacher to never call again, others become verbally abusive, and a few need to be escorted from the building. The other response is "nothing." Phone calls are not returned, nor will the parent come to the school to conference with the teacher, unless required by the principal to do so. For a *disruptive* student, many of their problems can be traced directly to their challenging home environment.

Low-Socioeconomic Students

This discussion focuses in large part on children from low-socioeconomic families and what educators can do to improve their academic progress. Of course, disruptive students are also present in many high-income schools and can be a major problem for the teachers to manage.

The following is a deeper look at some of the social realities of a disruptive student. Some live a very uncertain life outside of the classroom. For some, being at home is not a good thing. Some have been abused, some are homeless, and some have little or no support. Many times, there is no father in the picture and the mother is on welfare or working two maybe three jobs just to keep a roof over her family. As a result of these circumstances, student behaviors include:

1. They have a pronounced "I don't care" attitude, usually because they feel the people and institutions around them don't care about them
2. They do not respect others and certainly not their teachers
3. They are very difficult to manage in a classroom situation
4. Their parents often are not involved in many/any aspects of their educational growth
5. They do not exhibit an understanding of the value of an education
6. If a parent is contacted about a student issue and they agree to work with the student, it is often unusual for them to take any action

Because of these issues, test scores suffer for the entire classroom/school.

Teachers try to reach every child. Teachers eat with them, talk one-on-one with them, work with them and let them know that we genuinely care about them. The teachers see these kids for who they are and try to understand the issues they deal with day in and day out. Teachers know which students have parents going through divorce, which has a parent in jail or on welfare, or a child who has been beaten or abused.

Children are in school about 7 hours each day with only 220 minutes in instruction time with their teacher in their rooms. Considering an entire calendar year (365 days) the children are under the direct influence of their teachers and school about 14% of their time. With so many problem students, it is very hard for teachers to deal with the difficult and complicated issues that some of their students face.

Number of Students by Type

Once the definitions were finalized, each teacher was asked to estimate what percentage of their class was in the different categories. The display below gives the average for all four classes of each student type for 2012–2013:

Engaged 31%
Followers 46%
Disruptive 23%

Looking at these numbers, one begins to develop a better understanding of what a classroom is like for this D graded school. In a class of 24 to 25 students, there will be from 5 to 6 *disruptive* students. Because the *follower* students are more highly influenced by the *disruptives* than they are by the *engaged* they will, on occasion, fall into the *disruptive* category. This means that at times, the classroom could be composed of a majority of *disruptives*. These situations lead to classroom chaos and severely test the teacher's patience and endurance, plus result in dramatic reductions in classroom instruction time.

Picture yourself as a teacher in one of these classrooms. Teaching has appeal as a profession because of how much influence a teacher can have in a child's life. Early on, the profession sounds wonderful with a perfect mix of service and teaching. Soon it is discovered that far too little time is spent teaching. Often, there is the feeling that the classroom is in a constant state of upheaval because it is so difficult to control some of the students. This is a terrible morale-killer; with the teacher thinking, "There must be a way out of this school."

Which schools will support teaching and have good discipline? Are there schools where the teachers have a say in how things are done? Which schools engage parents to make the school better? Will it ever happen at this school? This may be the time to give up teaching and look for a better skill fit. The National Education Association reports that 33% of new teachers leave the profession in three years; 46% leave in five years.

Was 2012–2013 an Unusual Year?

The 2012–2013 (note this is the next year's fourth-grade class) third-grade teachers were asked to review the definitions of the different types of students and to break out the percentage of three kinds of students. The two years are almost identical in the percentages of the different types. So, the school year that was used in the study was typical; illustrating that these teachers face these situations for multiple years.

Examples of Disruptive Student Behaviors

Is it the students or is it the teacher? Below are some examples of *disruptive* student behavior from the press, studies, and so forth. Make up your own mind if a teacher should be expected to control this kind of behavior. *Keep in mind that these examples are not from the target school of the study team.* Many of these stories are about older children; well beyond the fourth grade. As the children grow older the events grow far more serious.

1. "He was mad at me because I made him redo a math test, so he walked over to the classroom door. When I told him I would need to call the office if he left the room without permission, he proceeded to slam his own leg in the door about five times, then he looked at me and said, 'Now my leg hurts and I'm going to tell everyone it was your fault'"[11]

2. "He was 5 and in kindergarten. I watched him at recess walk over to another boy and punch him in the face. With no emotion on his face. No feelings. When I found out who the kid was, turns out his grandfather went to prison for murdering a lot of prostitutes."[12]

3. "Then, suddenly, (and this sounds like it was pre-planned and done with military-style execution), this lone kid got up and stood on the table and started singing 'It's Oh So Quiet' by Björk. The teacher stood there in bemusement and confusion wondering what the hell was going on, until the bit where they sang the line 'and so peaceful until' Next thing, the whole class just went berserk and absolutely ransacked the classroom, forcing the teacher to flee, and the lesson got abandoned. I heard the classroom literally got destroyed as the kids went on the rampage."[13]

4. "Scores of teachers in Western Pennsylvania are the targets of assaults by students each year, according to state data."

5. "We need to recognize teaching is a hazardous occupation," said Dorothy Espelage, a professor of counseling and educational psychology at the University of Illinois at Urbana-Champaign.

6. "In February 2012, she saw a student throw another boy against a locker and begin beating him on the floor. She crouched down behind the 14-year-old and told him to stop. 'I knew the kid. I had him in class, and I knew when he gets emotionally upset, he gets physical,' said Swigart, who was a seventh-grade math teacher. 'He reached up and grabbed me by the neck and flipped me over his shoulder, and I wound up on the floor between them.' Swigart, who was 51 at the time, suffered a concussion and a shoulder injury. She was out of school about four weeks while she recovered."

7. A Philadelphia high school teacher was hospitalized in December when two students beat him in a dispute over a cell phone.

8. An experienced kindergarten teacher from Racine, Wisconsin, reviewed the draft paper (the one about working in a school graded D) and said the definitions of student types was appropriate for her *kindergarten* children. She once had a student who bashed a fellow student's head against a urinal and the child needed stitches.

9. A Memphis, Tennessee, teacher relates this story. Once student behavior reached a new low in a local middle school, she quit her job. She was verbally abused by the students, called gay, lesbian, a dyke, and even white girl. Students said this to her: "Who the f-bomb do you think you're talking to? And shut the F..k up." No punishment was given to any student for this behavior.

10. List of violent classroom episodes from YouTube videos.
    https://www.youtube.com/watch?v=hllCSqHPI_g
    https://www.youtube.com/watch?v=CLmQlKdhRO0

https://www.youtube.com/watch?v=-1eUADIdHWU
https://www.youtube.com/watch?v=Gg_44_cIjEM
https://www.youtube.com/watch?v=-1eUADIdHWU
https://www.youtube.com/watch?v=-1eUADIdHWU

According to a recent article published by the American Psychologist[14] (APA), *80% of teachers surveyed were victimized at school at least once in the current school year or prior year*. Violence against teachers is a "national crisis," according to Dr. Dorothy Espelage of the University of Illinois at Urbana-Champaign, who served as chair of the APA task force on Classroom Violence Directed at Teachers. And yet, the issue is generally ignored or at least underreported by the media and given inadequate attention by scholars—a deficiency that has widespread implications for school safety, the teaching profession and student learning.

About half of the teachers who reported being victimized experienced harassment. Others reported property offenses, including theft and damage to property. And about one-quarter of these teachers experienced physical attacks. Harassment includes anything from obscene gestures, verbal threats and intimidation and obscene remarks. With physical offenses, teachers widely reported objects being thrown at them and being physically attacked. The most severe and uncommon cases are physical attacks that result in a visit to the doctor.

Measuring Lost Time

When the teachers describe a typical day with all their interruptions two things are apparent:

1. Considerable classroom instructional time is wasted dealing with repeated instructions, getting the students' attention, and conduct.
2. The "learning environment" in the classroom is not good, particularly when the *disruptive* students can be so impactful.

Measuring—Gathering Data

The second step of the process is to gather data—as is said in industry, "speak with data." Data is objective and will eliminate a lot of the possible confusion in describing the magnitude of the problem to others. To this end, the school's teachers set up a measurement system to quantify the "lost instructional time."

To illustrate the nature of the classroom management challenge, the teachers set up a group of three metrics and data was gathered. These three metrics are easy to track, and daily data was collected for two to three weeks, a total of 44 classroom days. The metrics are:

1. Multiple requests to follow directions
2. Failure to actively listen
3. Bad attitude/conflict

Loss of Instruction Time

Two items of data are needed to quantify instructional lost time:

1. How often does a disruption occur?
2. Once the classroom is disrupted, how long does it take to return to the normal instructional mode?

Dealing with number 2 first leads to interesting and very important concepts.

As the teachers contemplated these estimates, discussion targeted the framework in which the teachers should position their thinking. The classroom has settled down, and the entire classroom is in an instructional mode, that is, in the "learning groove." Suddenly there is an outburst of anger by one of the students. Everything stops, the students raise their heads to listen and observe the disruption; the teacher immediately leaves instructional mode and enters a disciplinary mode.

Minutes later the disruption seems to be over, and the students go back to work. Are the students at this point able to focus on learning or will more time have to pass before the class is truly back into an instructional mode? The teachers were asked to estimate the time from the beginning of the disturbance to the return of the apparent instructional mode. Certainly, this is not easy to do. However, estimates were made and subsequently used to estimate the minutes of classroom time lost each day to interruptions.

Table 6.1 shows the time estimates the teachers selected for the duration of each of the three types of classroom disruptions:

Table 6.1. Teacher's Estimates of the Length of a Disruption

Teacher's Estimates of the Length of a Disruption	
Measured Disruption	Instructional Time Lost in Minutes per Event
Multiple requests to follow directions	.5
Failure to actively listen	.25
Bad attitude/conflict	4.5

Now what is needed is the average daily count for each disruption type. Using clipboards and tally marks, the teachers made these estimates. The data in table 6.2 was gathered over 44 classroom days (all four teachers).

Table 6.2. Daily Average Distractions of a Typical Classroom (Total Tally Marks Are Averaged per Day per Class)

Daily Average Distractions for Typical Classroom The total tally marks are averaged per day per class			
	Multiple requests to follow directions	Failure to actively listen	Bad attitude/conflict
Overall Average	26	11	10

To find the total average lost instructional time per day, simply multiply the duration of the event by the number of times it occurs per day. Here are the results of this multiplication:

Table 6.3. How Much Time Is Lost Each Day to Classroom Disruptions? (Table Shows the Result of the Time Lost Each Day)

How much time is lost each day to Classroom Disruptions? This table shows the result of the time lost each day.			
Measured Disruption	Time Loss Per Event	Average Number of Events per Day	Total in Minutes
Multiple requests to follow directions	.5	26	13
Failure to actively listen	.25	11	3
Bad attitude/conflict	4.5	10.23	46
		Total Lost Time for Each Classroom Each Day	62 min.

Each day, in each classroom, the teacher must deal with 62 minutes of lost instruction time, 46 minutes of which comes from disciplinary problems from disruptive children.

Table 6.3 points out that the three measured classroom management issues take away 62 minutes from the 220-minute instructional day; this is a 28% (62 min/220 min of instruction) drop in instructional time, a loss that no student can afford. (On an annual basis, this is about 186 hours of lost instruction time.) This time loss, and the associated classroom disruptions, do not contribute to a healthy or positive "learning environment."

This lost time is one of the major reasons more of these students did not do well on their assessment exams, especially with the teachers saying they could be successful. Look at a typical 5-day week at school. These children are in classes where 28% of the time is lost. So instead of 5 days of instruction, they receive 3.6. It's no wonder test scores are so low!

As extra supporting information, a highly respected retired principal of two elementary schools in Lawrence Township, Indianapolis, Indiana, reviewed this estimation process and made this comment: *"The 62 minutes of lost instructional time is too low."*

This improved time availability, along with a much-improved learning environment, will provide the impetus needed to excel on the standardized exams. The teachers believe that this is one of the primary root causes for the classes' poor test performance. There is also a major psychological consideration that will be beneficial. The engaged and the follower students are amenable to learning. What are they thinking about their desire to learn when the teacher and the administration allow so much disruption and loss of time in the classroom?

ROOT CAUSES

The study team's search process for determining root causes of classroom disruption uncovered these three:

1. Parents/parenting—Parents of disruptive students have not imparted to them the needed noncognitive skills nor the motivation to become better educated.
2. Cultural—There are cultural biases in some ethnic groups that do not admire and sometime denigrate intellectual capabilities.
3. Choice—The students have made the choice to be disruptive in the classroom.

Regarding student choice, in many cases the disruption is a deliberate strategy to prevent learning. The more time the students can waste, the less they must remember, the less homework that will be assigned, and the fewer questions that can be asked on an exam. In discussions with teachers, they agree that this is a prevalent student strategy.

A Speech Relevant to Root Cause 2 Above

Here is a portion of Michelle Obama's 2013 Commencement Address at Bowie State University, Prince George's County, Maryland:

> But today, more than 150 years after the Emancipation Proclamation, more than 50 years after the end of "separate but equal," when it comes to getting an education, too many of our young people just can't be bothered. Today, instead of walking miles every day to school, they're sitting on couches for hours playing video games, watching TV. Instead of dreaming of being a teacher or a lawyer or a business leader, they're fantasizing about being a baller or a rapper.
>
> (Applause.) Right now, one in three African American students are dropping out of high school. Only one in five African Americans between the ages of 25 and 29 has gotten a college degree—one in five.
>
> It is that kind of unwavering determination; that relentless focus on getting an education in the face of obstacles, that's what we need to reclaim, as a community and as a nation. That was the idea at the very heart of the founding of this school.
>
> So, I think we can agree, and we need to start feeling that hunger again, you know what I mean? (Applause.) We need to once again fight to educate ourselves and our children like our lives depend on it, because they do.[15]

Can Parents Be Held Responsible for Their Disruptive Child?

If the parents are one of the root causes of the behavior of their disruptive child, is it possible to make them legally responsible? There are some instances where this is the case. Note, this article also gives a dissenting opinion.

> The new law in Virginia that would impose penalties for parents when their children misbehave in school ("Parents in Va. Face Fines for Unruly Pupils," front page, May 6) is a great improvement to the state's educational system. This strict new law serves to punish those parents who choose to take a passive role in controlling their children's behavior. It is widely known that children behave better when their parents play an active role in their lives.
>
> By reprimanding irresponsible parents through expensive fines, this law will discourage the neglect that some parents choose to show their children and correct parents' unwillingness to deal directly with any problems. It is fortunate for the people of Virginia that their state legislature efficiently produced legislation that will, I hope, discourage the behavior that is so detrimental to learning in the schools.
>
> Virginia is to be commended for its fast action in preparing this law, which is to be implemented in the fall. It should serve as a model for school systems throughout the country. (From: Dariush Afshar, Washington)

[Here is the dissenting opinion:]

I don't think that getting tough with parents is the answer to disciplining children who misbehave in school. Such laws have been tried before without much success.

It would make more sense to get tougher on the troublemakers themselves. By this I don't mean to punish the kids by suspending them, either in or out of school. That is a waste of time. Punishments should take the form of doing productive things, such as community service after school and on weekends. This way, students still can have the privilege of education during the week.

I realize that parents need to take some responsibility, but laws like this one are not the answer. Better to send notices to parents of misbehaving students, followed up by phone calls, demanding a response in a certain period of time. The only time I think it would be effective to fine the parents would be when property has been damaged. Sending the parents to jail would only give the kids less time to spend with their parents. (From: Mauricio Gutierrez, Rockville)[16]

Mauricio Gutierrez, the dissenting voice in this piece, is terribly naive about what is going on in today's classrooms. Send notes home and follow up with a phone call. In many classrooms this will not change anything. Many parents don't care.

Here is what the State of Illinois has been doing, also with some quick action by the state that reversed it. The State Superintendent tries to stop the practice.

Illinois law bans schools from fining students. So local police are doing it for them, issuing thousands of tickets a year for truancy, vaping, fights, and other misconduct. Children are then thrown into a legal system designed for adults.

Update, April 29, 2022: Hours after the publication of this investigation on April 28, Illinois State Board of Education Superintendent Carmen Ayala urged school administrators across the state to stop working with police to ticket students, saying fines associated with the tickets hurt families and there's no evidence they change students' behavior.[17]

Here is a different kind of action against parents when the children do not attend school.

Penalties for Parents of Truant Students

Because parents are legally responsible for making sure their children go to school, they could face misdemeanor charges for violating Indiana's compulsory education laws. But prosecutors may not file criminal charges until the parent has received official notice of the violation and the child hasn't returned to school by the following day. Convictions bring mandatory jail time (up to 180 days), along with potential fines (up to $1,000) for each day of violation.

Articles like this that involve truancy are quite common in the literature so punishing parents for their child missing school is nothing new.

Proposal for Corrective Action

Finally, after reviewing data that estimates the impact of disruptive children on instruction time, what actions should be considered? Here is a proposal. Looking only at the disruptive children, divide them into two groups:

Disruptive 1 (D1) these are students who will be grouped into classes with a low teacher to student ratio and taught like any other group but with methods especially designed for this type of student.

Disruptive 2 (D2) these students were assigned to a D1 class, but, over time, they are so disruptive that they are expelled from school until such a time that they prove to the administration they are ready to return.

Implementing a D1 Class

Just like the report reviewed from Public Agenda, it is suggested that the most disruptive students be removed from the school. They will not be "written off" but be placed in an environment that will expand upon what they learn and how they do it. They need a different mix of instruction, one rich in non-cognitive skills as well as cognitive skills.[18]

Here is an example of how to set up special class for disruptives. In the case of the four fourth grades mentioned earlier, there are a total of 4 classes of 24 students, or 96 students in total. Twenty-three percent of these are *disruptive* students so a class of 22 *disruptives* is established and three classes of 24–25 others, the *engaged* and the *followers*.

Figure 6.1 is a pictorial to illustrate the new configuration and here are the six essentials for the new class:

1. Emphasize/teaches character and grit.
2. Utilize discipline as a teaching tool.
3. Values are taught and ingrained into all students.
4. Provides an environment of fellowship and camaraderie—something they are missing at home.
5. Has a substantial amount of caring adult intervention.
6. Continue to teach the required course material.

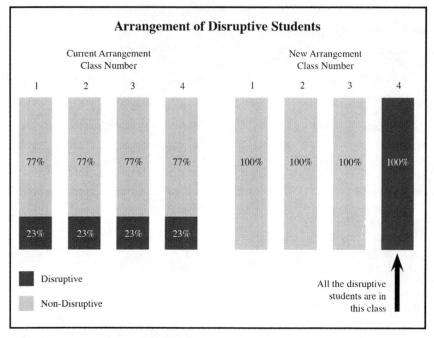

Figure 6.1. Arrangement of Disruptive Students

The new class will probably need to be taught by two caring adults who have the experience and talent to manage these difficult students. Since the restoration of hope in a child[19] is keyed to the presence of caring adults, two caring adults will do a better job.

Another important feature of this configuration is that the other three classes can be taught by "ordinary" teachers who do not have to waste valuable minutes of instructional time maintaining order. This will boost staff morale for these individuals, and it will allow them to recapture the joy of teaching.

Advice From an Expert

After bringing up an early website, contact was made with an experienced teacher who taught difficult children in inner city schools. Her name was Janice Minion. The teaching profession does not have many teachers with skills to teach the *disruptive* students. Ms. Minion could do this job well. Hopefully, her advice will assist other teachers.

Janice Minion (she has passed away) was an experienced teacher who taught challenging students in inner city schools of Houston, Texas, for 18 years. She was a summa cum laude graduate of the University of Pittsburgh with a major in education and was incredibly serious about teaching. She worked many years in education, but not all of those years were in a classroom. For example, she worked for Johns Hopkins for six years advocating for their reading program across the nation.

In her first year of teaching, she willingly accepted the responsibility to teach a grade exactly like Class 4 in the diagram above. She wanted the challenge of working with these children so badly in need of an education. She did this for 18 years and felt a great deal of satisfaction with her success. Not a single child she taught was beyond her patience or her ability to teach. She produced successful students. Her teaching is yet another example of the hope talked about in this book. These students can learn!

She had outstanding diagnostic skills and could come up with teaching techniques that overcome the deficiencies of the approach normally used in schools. She applied her great intellectual skills where they were needed, in the classroom.

Best Ideas of an Experienced Teacher, Janice Minion

At the beginning of the school year, place the students on two-person teams. Put the best student with the worst student, the next best with the next worst and so on. Here are some of the advantages:

1. The better student benefits from helping the weaker student in that they explain concepts, aid with reading, etc. This help reinforces their skills.
2. The weaker student benefits from hearing their peer explain ideas; the uptake here is in the range of 69%, which is considerably above the retention from a lecture (in the range of 6%). In addition, advice from the partner can be repeated whenever needed.
3. Questions, complements, and admonitions are aimed at the team and not an individual. This shelters individual students from negative recognition, which was one of her important goals.

This may look like a one-way street with information and insights only moving from the brighter student to the teammate, but this is not the case; it will be a two-way street. It follows the adage, if you want to learn something, teach it.

The Ten Points

1. Build self-esteem. The key is to make the student feel successful. This point is at the head of the list because it is, by far, the most important item.

2. Require the students to exhibit reading skills in all topics. Everything is reading; spelling is reading, language is reading, science and social studies is reading, and so forth.
3. Use hands-on experiments to teach science. Ms. Minion says that a student "would walk five miles in the snow if they knew a science lesson was going to be a hands-on experiment."
4. Never skip spelling or language. Young children at this age can pronounce many words, but many times they do not know the meaning of the words. Spelling not only produces the proper sequence of letters but it adds words to their vocabulary.
5. Math is the easiest to teach. The essence of teaching math is to move knowledge from short-term to long-term memory. Every day, before the math lesson, the students work on ten problems they have already seen: maybe not the exact same problem but similar. This repeat work helps to lodge the older knowledge in long-term memory. Classroom grades are only given to individual students; teams are not graded.
6. Only reward students for *wanted* behavior. Do not publicly recognize their negatives. Reward a student team when something good happens. Calling out a student's name for bad behavior gives the student recognition for the wrong reason. If a student is misbehaving, Minion will stand by their side with a stern look on her face and if that does not work, she whispers for them to behave.
7. Give spelling tests. Every Friday the students are given the weekly spelling test. On Thursday, the teacher gives a spelling pretest on the words that will be on the Friday exam. If a student receives a 100% on the Thursday pretest, they do not have to take the Friday exam. Their reward is they are free to do whatever they want (quietly) during the Friday exam.
8. When reading something short and low level, for example, *The Three Little Pigs*, ask questions that develop higher level learning; questions that go well beyond the story itself.
9. Model handwriting. If writing on the board or overhead, let them watch the writing take place.
10. On Friday, the teacher celebrates the successes of the week. The teacher tells them to give themselves a pat on the back. She tells the students to enjoy their weekend and asks all of them to come to class on Monday with smiles and enthusiasm.

Chapter 7 will focus on character and grit as well as social-emotional learning. Character and grit or social-emotional learning are the antidotes to discipline problems. For the student to begin better behavior and thus more learning, these skills must be imparted early in their school lives. This book advocates beginning instruction for the more at-risk children at age 3. The teaching of these skills should begin at this age so the issue of discipline will be much smaller later.

The worst of the worst students should be expelled. Most of us believe that free public education is a right given by the U.S. Constitution. This is not the case. No mention is made of education in any of the amendments. However, the 10th Amendment states that powers not delegated to the federal government are reserved to the states or to the people. Thus, education is a function of the state rather than the federal government though there is a lot of federal involvement.

Here is the Indiana law. "Section 1. Knowledge and learning, generally diffused throughout a community, being essential to the preservation of a free government; it shall be the duty of the General Assembly to encourage, by all suitable means, moral, intellectual, scientific, and agricultural improvement; and to provide, by law, for a general and uniform system of Common Schools, wherein tuition shall be without charge, and equally open to all."

There appears to be no mention of the right of the state to expel students who are, by their disruptive actions, destroying their classes and demoralizing their teachers. The discipline problem long ago reached the point where this action should have already been common.

This ends the discussion on U.S. disciplinary issues. Since very little of past practices have worked, it is time to try something else. Hopefully, the suggestions from this chapter will help. Implementing the special classes for disruptive students will cost money but without them nothing changes and the U.S. falls further behind.

NOTES

1. This is the author's website and was intended to be another book, more interesting, multimedia than an ordinary. However, the public has yet to discover its virtues.

2. Levings, Kenton, "Classroom Management: The Most Common Mistakes and How to Avoid Them," Insights to Behavior, September 26, 2020, https://insightstobehavior.com/blog/classroom-management-common-mistakes-avoid/

3. Rosemond, John, "Discipline, a Problem in Schools in America," AP Trending News, February 12, 2019, https://apnews.com/article/1ea06dcba5b24a4a9fa2c807eda2d112

4. This section is an excerpt from my book, *The Kids Are Smart Enough, So What's the Problem? A Businessman's Perspective on Educational Reform and the Teacher Crisis*, Rowman & Littlefield, 2017.

5. *Teaching Interrupted: Do Discipline Policies in Today's Public Schools Foster the Common Good?*, Public Agenda with support from Common Good, May 2004, https://files.eric.ed.gov/fulltext/ED485312.pdf

6. Ibid.

7. Ibid.

8. Ibid.

9. Ibid.

10. Ibid.

11. Behman, Elizabeth, "Classroom in Crisis: Violence Plagues Schools," *TRIB Live*, January 10, 2016.

12. Ibid.

13. Ibid.

14. Espelage, Dorothy, et al. "Understanding and Preventing Violence Directed Against Teachers," *American Psychologist*, March 2013, Vol. 68, no. 2, pp. 75–87.

15. Source: http://www.whitehouse.gov/the-press-office/2013/05/17/remarks-first -lady-bowie-state-university-commencement-ceremony

16. Gutierrez, Mauricio, "Punishing Parents for Student Behavior," *Washington Post*, May 1995, https://www.washingtonpost.com/archive/opinions/1995 /05/19/punishing-parents-for-students-misbehavior/02a9b37d-1e45-452f-942e -c23d085b94e7/

17. Cohen, Jodi S., Richards-Smith, Jennifer, Sanchez, Armando, "The Price Kids Pay: Schools and Police Punish Students with Costly Tickets for Minor Misbehavior," April 28, https://www.propublica.org/article/illinois-school-police-tickets-fines

18. Gielten, E. A., "What Happens to Truants and Their Parents in Indiana?," *Education Law*, August 21, 2019, https://www.lawyers.com/legal-info/research/education -law/what-happens-to-truants-and-their-parents-in-indiana.html

19. Garrett, Richard, op.cit., pp. 25–29.

Chapter 7

The Success Equation for Children

LOOKING FOR ROOT CAUSE[1]

Why aren't our students performing better? Answer, too much classroom time is wasted due to discipline issues. Why is classroom discipline so unmanageable? Answer: the students are lacking certain noncognitive skills, such as how to compromise, how to avoid conflict, and receive respect. One camp calls the missing skills character and grit, another calls the missing skills social and emotional learning. Why are students lacking these noncognitive skills? The answer is the topic of this chapter.

It would be easy to stop at this point and simply find someone to blame but this would be stopping too early in our quest for the root cause. The teachers wanted to stop here and blame the parents but no, these children are different from the other kids. What is different? The "Why" question is, why are the disruptive students unruly and such a problem in class?

The teachers agree that they do not possess certain socio-emotional and motivation skills that are usually taken for granted, and if they do have the appropriate skills, they are hiding them while in the classroom. For example, when undertaking even a simple task the children just quit without even trying. They are lacking grit.

Here is the list of skills the teachers say the *disruptive* students are lacking:

- Understanding that education is essential for them to lead a better life.
- Understanding that even though their circumstances may be far from ideal, they can still be successful if they believe in their teachers and their role in teaching them essential skills.
- Understanding why respect of others is so essential for their own success.
- Understanding the need to learn how to manage the behaviors that are brought about because of their life situation.

- Understanding the importance of self-discipline and self-motivation.
- Understanding what language is acceptable and what is profane and unacceptable.
- Understanding how to deal with conflict and how to avoid inflicting either mental or physical harm upon others.
- Learning the virtue of perseverance and its importance—learning can be hard work.

THE HIGH-LEVEL ATTRIBUTES OF
CHARACTER AND GRIT

In 2012, Paul Tough penned an excellent book titled, *How Children Succeed: Grit, Curiosity, and the Hidden Power of Character*. Here is a summary of his great book:

> *How Children Succeed* introduces us to a new generation of researchers and educators who, for the first time, are using the tools of science to peel back the mystery of character. Through their stories—and the stories of children they are trying to help—Tough traces the links between childhood stress and life success. He uncovers the surprising way parents do—and do not—prepare their children for adulthood. And he provides us with new insights into how to help children growing up in poverty.[2]

A social scientist working on this issue is James Heckman, an economist at the University of Chicago. Heckman shared the Nobel Memorial Prize in Economics in 2000 with Daniel McFadden for their pioneering work in econometrics and microeconomics. He is among the most influential economists in the world and is referenced in Tough's best-selling book.

For years, Dr. Heckman has studied, written about, and talked about the essential importance of noncognitive skills (socio-emotional skills, including character and grit) to success in life. He is a strong advocate of early intervention in the lives of underprivileged children who, if not raised in a loving, caring family will have difficulties in both the cognitive and the noncognitive skills.

In 2012, Paul Tough produced a best-selling book titled *How Children Succeed*[3] that has influenced readers around the world. This book has been translated into 25 different languages. His writing brings Professor Heckman's, and other researchers' work, into the popular media and makes it great reading for millions of people concerned about how we're educating our children.

A 20-minute video of his summary of the book is available on the website, www.elevateteachers.org. Go to Lesson 20 to view.

Following Heckman's work, author Tough separates the elements of success into two kinds of abilities. The first is the cognitive abilities. These skills have to do with the acquisition of knowledge, critical thinking skills, problem solving abilities, and so forth. These are the topics traditionally taught in the school systems.

The second set of skills Tough labels as character and grit—these are the noncognitive skills emphasized by Heckman. Tough points out that both sets of skills/values are important; in some instances the intellectual skills top the character and grit attributes but in other cases it is the other way around. Much of what is accomplished in the world is derived from character and grit.

HERE ARE SOME EXAMPLES TO BETTER DEFINE CHARACTER AND GRIT

Grit is passion and perseverance for a long-term goal. It includes having stamina, working hard to make the future a reality, and living life as a marathon.

Character is a person's pattern of behavior, thoughts, and feelings that are based on sound principles, moral judgments, integrity and the "line you never cross." Character education is generally in two parts: "performance character" (maximizing one's performance in every area of his or her life) and "moral character" (always choosing to do the right, honest and ethical thing).

Character and grit can be described using seven high-level attributes:

1. Curiosity
2. Gratitude
3. Zest
4. Optimism
5. Self-control
6. Social intelligence
7. Grit

Each of the skills disruptive students lack can be positioned under one of these higher-level attributes. This is the basis for the conclusion that they are lacking in character and grit.

Remember that life skills are learned just like knowledge skills. These skills are taken for granted because children usually learn them a little at a time over many years; skills they are taught by the people who raised them, along with neighbors, coaches, teachers, and friends. So, the teachers report that there is a major shortfall in these skills that need to be addressed. Is it too early to expect a fourth grader to be able to change behavior? The teachers don't think so. It would be very beneficial to the student, future classrooms, and society if they could gain more successful noncognitive skills earlier in their lives.

THE SUCCESS EQUATION

Figure 7.1 is an equation that combines school-produced "book learning" with the more elusive noncognitive skills of character and grit or social-emotional skills. As has already been discussed, without hope this equation does not work. *The creation of hope is a necessary prerequisite; the key element in generating hope is caring adults.*

WHAT CHILDREN NEED TO BE SUCCESSFUL

Looking at how human endeavors are accomplished, too many times success is attributed to "brainpower" when in fact, brainpower, all by itself, accomplishes very little. There are many brilliant people who accomplish well below their potential because they do not have the persistence to set and reach long-term goals. On the other hand, many can overcome shortfalls in intellect by simply "trying harder." There is a one-way substitution between intellect and grit.

Grit can substitute for intellect.
Intellect cannot be a substitute for grit.

For a young fourth grader, it is essential that they possess character and grit not just to produce success when they are 30 years old, but so they can be successful in class tomorrow and the day after and so on. They must develop a

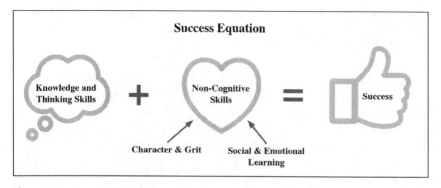

Figure 7.1.   Success Equation

longer-term vision for which to strive, to have a reason to perform on exams, do homework and to actively participate in class. Teachers attribute a lack of character and grit for the unacceptable behavior of a proportion of each of their classes, the *disruptive* children.

CHARACTER AND GRIT BUILDS SELF-ESTEEM

A by-product of a program that produces character and grit is self-esteem. A child with character and grit has their "act together" and can carry their heads high because they have the inner strength it requires to be in full control of themselves. They know how to deal with failure, and they have the pride of knowing that they "measure up" with anyone.

IS THE CHARACTER/GRIT FACTOR A REDISCOVERY?

In years past, when the social structure was significantly different, and more family-focused, the development of character and grit was taken for granted. Children came from two-parent families where both parents focused on the family, assigned chores/tasks to their children, and molded the children's character and grit.

Today, the world has changed dramatically. The traditional family structure has changed in several ways:

1. Many families have two working adults.
2. Many poor children live with a single parent, or with grandparents, or other relatives.
3. Sometimes the single parent lacks the skills to compete for a well-paying job—and must work multiple jobs to support the most meager lifestyle.
4. Many families are on welfare and are part of the multigenerational poor.
5. Children are engaged in after-class events to bolster résumés rather than teach employable skills.
6. Millions of low- and middle-income manufacturing jobs have been exported to low labor cost countries or replaced with automation; this hurts family income and spirit.
7. The influence of the church is waning as fewer and fewer people attend.
8. Our media culture molds thinking as to how a family should live, what they should eat and wear, creating illusions that bring about discontent in some situations. A good example is footwear; if it is not expensive it isn't worth wearing.

9. There is a "I want it now" attitude in some young people—this is defeat-
   ing the ability to patiently work to accomplish a difficult task.

These changes have inadvertently suppressed the role of character and grit
in the lives of young people.

WHERE DOES SOCIAL-EMOTIONAL LEARNING FIT?

Once defined, it will be clear that social-emotional learning is targeting the
second term in the success equation, the noncognitive piece. This part of the
equation has three possible teaching approaches:

1. Character and grit
2. Social-emotional learning (SEL)
3. Some combination of 1 and 2. For example SEL + Grit

What is social-emotional learning (SEL)? Here is a definition from the
Washington Post.

> Social-emotional learning (SEL) programs are intended to help people learn
> and effectively use "knowledge, attitudes and skills necessary to understand
> and manage emotions, set and achieve positive goals, feel and show empathy
> for others, establish and maintain positive relationships, and make responsible
> decisions."[4]

Andy Hargreaves and Dennis Shirley, both professors at Boston College,
comment on the SEL movement into our schools:

> A broad movement is tearing through our schools. Many teachers love it.
> Professional developers can't get enough of it. Systems are investing heavily in
> it. Finally, it seems, schools can focus on something else other than test scores
> and technology: our children's emotional and mental health. It's called social
> and emotional learning, or SEL for short.
>   SEL is aimed at developing skills that enable young people to understand
> and express their own and each other's emotions, manage feelings, learn
> self-regulation, and build positive relationships. SEL has become a front-line
> effort to battle the mental health epidemic that is plaguing our young people.[5]

SEL is targeted for students of all ages beginning with PreK. Most renditions
of SEL point out there are five areas of focus for this concept, and curriculum
material available to convert these topics into lessons.

The Five Core SEL Competencies[6]

1. Self-Awareness
2. Self-Management
3. Social Awareness
4. Relationship Skills
5. Responsible Decision Making

Self-awareness is the ability to understand one's own emotions, thoughts, and values and how they influence behavior across contexts. This includes capacities to recognize one's strengths and limitations with a well-grounded sense of confidence and purpose.

Self-management is the ability to manage one's emotions, thoughts, and behaviors effectively in different situations and to achieve goals and aspirations. This includes the capacities to delay gratification, manage stress, and feel motivation and agency to accomplish personal and collective goals.

Social awareness is the ability to understand the perspectives of and empathize with others, including those from diverse backgrounds, cultures, and contexts. This includes the capacities to feel compassion for others, understand broader historical and social norms for behavior in different settings, and recognize family, school, and community resources and supports.

Relationship skills are the ability to establish and maintain healthy and supportive relationships and to effectively navigate settings with diverse individuals and groups. This includes the capacities to communicate clearly, listen actively, cooperate, work collaboratively to problem solve and negotiate conflict constructively, navigate settings with differing social and cultural demands and opportunities, provide leadership, and seek or offer help when needed.

Responsible decision-making is the ability to make caring and constructive choices about personal behavior and social interactions across diverse situations. This includes the capacities to consider ethical standards and safety concerns, and to evaluate the benefits and consequences of various actions for personal, social, and collective well-being.

Here is a summary wrap-up from the Harvard Graduate School of Education:

The field of social and emotional learning (SEL) is rapidly expanding. Over the past two decades, there has emerged a growing consensus among researchers who study child development, education, and health that social and emotional skills are essential to learning and life outcomes. Furthermore, research indicates that high-quality, evidence-based programs and policies that promote these skills among students can improve physical and mental wellbeing, academic outcomes, and college and career readiness and success.

Over the past two decades, SEL has emerged as an umbrella term for a few concepts, including non-cognitive development, character education, 21st century skills, and trauma-informed learning, among others. Researchers, educators, and policymakers alike are beset by dilemmas about what exactly is included in this broad domain. Popular press highlights skills such as grit, empathy, growth mindset, social skills, and more.

Yet while SEL programs typically target multiple skills, very few programs target all these skills. Furthermore, each program has its own way of building skills through specific teaching and learning activities, and its own programmatic components that define how the program looks and feels, as well as how skills are addressed and presented through explicit messages or implicit themes.

For example, some programs are focused on "character traits" such as honesty, while others focus on skills like understanding emotions and solving problems, or a core theme like identity development. Some programs use discussions as the primary learning activity, while others are movement-based or game-oriented. Some programs have extensive family engagement or teacher professional development components, while others have none. Some programs are designed to be highly flexible and adaptable to context, while others are scripted and uniform.

These differences matter to schools, families, out-of-school-time organizations, researchers, and policymakers because they signal differences in what gets taught and how. This report was designed to provide information about the specific features that define SEL programs and that may be important to stakeholders who are selecting, recommending, evaluating, or reporting on different SEL programs, or to those who are aligning efforts across multiple schools, programs, or regions.

At the same time, social, emotional, and behavioral factors are increasingly incorporated into education accountability metrics (e.g., *ESSA: Every Student Succeeds Act*), and school climate initiatives, anti-bullying work, positive behavior supports (e.g., PBIS), and discipline reform are increasingly influencing the day-to-day practice of schools and communities.

Moreover, as the United States grapples with the COVID-19 pandemic alongside the rest of the world, children and adults are either returning to or creating new learning environments that look and feel very different from what they are used to. Strong SEL supports are more critical than ever in this new learning climate to maintain strong and supportive relationships; build resiliency and coping skills; and support the social and emotional assets shown to buffer against the negative effects of trauma and stress.[7]

As a final act, contrast the character and grit items to the five SEL target areas. Character and grit can be described using seven high-level attributes and SEL by five competencies. Here they are side by side for comparison (see table 7.1).

Looking at these two columns, the right side is missing grit and none of the other competencies seem to include it. The SEL competencies are very social and seem to apply to group settings while the Character and Grit are more focused on individual personal traits.

Table 7.1. Contrasting the Character and Grit Attributes to the SEL Five Core
Competencies

Contrasting the Character and Grit Attributes to the SEL Five Core Competencies	
Character & Grit	*SEL Competencies*
Curiosity	Self-Awareness
Gratitude	Self-Management
Optimism	Social Awareness
Self-control	Relationship Skills
Social Intelligence	Responsible Decision-Making
Grit	

There is this important consideration to consider as this chapter closes. As the success equation illustrates, and as Paul Tough discusses, student success depends on two different skills, cognitive and noncognitive. It is imperative that both be a focus for an educational system. More of the responsibility for the noncognitive skills falls on the schools because some parents are not, for whatever reason, doing this job.

NOTES

1. This chapter is a blend of material from the author's previous book, *The Kids Are Smart Enough, So What's the Problem?* and new thoughts.
2. Tough, Paul, *How Children Succeed: Grit, Curiosity, and the Hidden Power of Character*, Houghton Mifflin Harcourt, 2012.
3. Ibid.
4. Strauss, Valerie, "Why Social-Emotional Learning Isn't Enough to Help Today," *Washington Post*, December 7, 2021, https://www.washingtonpost.com/education/2021/12/17/why-socialemotional-learning-isnt-enough/
5. Ibid.
6. Agular, Cap, Bridges, Carissa, "A Guide to the Core SEL Competencies (+ Activities and Strategies)," https://www.panoramaed.com/blog/guide-to-core-sel-competencies?utm_term=&utm_campaign=RLSA&utm_source=adwords&utm_medium=ppc&hsa_acc=5445977957&hsa_cam=17935108980&hsa_grp=141340114002&hsa_ad=614387631540

7. Jones, Stephanie M., et al., "Navigating SEL From the Inside Out: Preschool and Elementary Focus," *Harvard Graduate School of Education*, July 2021, https://www.wallacefoundation.org/knowledge-center/Documents/navigating-social-and-emotional-learning-from-the-inside-out-2ed.pdf

Chapter 8

How Should Schools Be Organized?

Before jumping into this chapter some points need to be laid out. First is the common idea that every U.S. high school graduate should attend a college or university. This is not reasonable; it is in fact folly, and it will not work for many reasons. This philosophy has played a role in curriculum planning for years, leading to a challenging math requirement that must be taken to graduate high school. The second idea deals with relevance. Students need to see relevance in their course of study and the sooner this can be established, the more motivated they become. Here is the proper restatement of what ought to happen when a student graduates:

Every high school graduate should either enter a university or obtain a professional school certificate.

This chapter draws on international school systems; it isn't any particular country, but an amalgamation of several top countries. It is based on the premise that individual student success is more important than group success. With good individual success, group success will be automatic.

Recall the analogy of the naval military convoy. What determines the speed of the entire group? The speed of the slowest ship! In this chapter, this concept is tossed out the window in favor of multiple convoys that move at different speeds. A design is presented that will provide individual success in such a way that group performance is also maximized. After all, groups don't go to college, individuals do, groups don't take industry jobs, individuals do. It's the training of each individual student that matters most.

This chapter is on tracking; the grouping of like skilled students into "small schools" within a bigger school.

In any group of students there will usually be a wide range of intellect, motivation, character, and general capabilities. Some learn quickly and others

71

do not. Some are very intelligent and others a bit slower. What is the best way to organize a school to maximize the individual student learning? There are two general options; the first option places more capable students into a "track" that will allow the teachers to offer more and deeper learning, more homework, and just get more done. Certainly, this track is for the "smart kids." This separation of students will upset some of the parents because their kids didn't make the cut. The second way to organize is to group all students together regardless of skill level.

The school employing tracking must offer all students a good option. Indeed, there can be several different tracks; what is vital is that every child has a track that matches their interests and abilities.

Here is a sports analogy to illuminate this situation. You have a child that is a gifted basketball player; gifted in the sense that they are the best player on the team and might even be honored with conference first-team placement. Where should they attend college and play basketball?

An NCAA Division 1 top school might be a possibility and they may be able to make it on one of the teams, but here is the issue. Make the Duke team and spend their career on the bench helping the first team get better by challenging them in practice and possibly win postseason games but never playing. The other option would be to make a lesser Division 1 team, say Evansville University, and be a star player with many playing minutes.

In a top student track, a slower student will indeed be in the track, but at the bottom of the list;. On the other hand, in a track that is close to track 1, but is not the top track, the student will fit in a lot better. They are a competitor, highly motivated, and can hold their own with anyone on that track. Between these two options where will the student learn the most?

On the other hand, when students of every ability are grouped together, there is not a banner for the gifted student to wear that says, "I am a top student." The student is just one of the guys. What happens now? If the teacher tries to speed up instruction and cover the required topics to keep the motivated students engaged, some of the students need special attention and this slows the class down.

Using the slowest ship in the convoy analogy, will the motivated students' presence in class stimulate the slower students and will help them learn? Perhaps, but there is no obligation for the top students to sacrifice their learning to boost others.

Now take the role of an average student. In a tracked system, suppose they accidentally end up on track 1. They might be motivated more in this group to work very hard to keep up and you might rise to the occasion. They have always had latent ability but never the motivation to pull out all the stops and give it a good go. On the other hand, they may find themselves woefully outclassed and very uncomfortable.

Now consider the second option: everyone together in the same class. Here the competition is not so tough. There are some very bright students in the room, but also other students who are willing to concede the high ground to them and aim for a "B" or a "C." In fact, the better students may earn all the high grades, leaving no "A's" for anyone else. In the basketball analogy, they get the playing time, and the others are on the bench.

In a good tracking scheme, there must be mobility between tracks. If a student thinks they can perform satisfactorily in another track, they petition to be moved. After consultation between child, parents, teachers, and school administrators a decision is made, and a trial period begins. From this point on, it's up to the student to prove they belong on the new track.

THE RECOMMENDED TRACKING SCHEME

Figure 8.1 is a graphic depicting a four-track high school system. Students in most advanced countries complete what the U.S. calls high school in 10 years. As has been seen, the U.S. takes 12 and still doesn't do a very good job. This is a unique point about this graphic; high school is over in 10 years for the top three tracks, but graduation is still two years away. In this graphic, all but track 4 end at 10 years for ordinary high school classes; the last track continues until the end of year 12. If the schools are small, tracks 1 and 2 can be merged.

Students are assigned to their appropriate track based on test scores, past class performance and faculty approval. This will be a bone of contention for some parents, but the schools must firmly plant their flags to assure that only

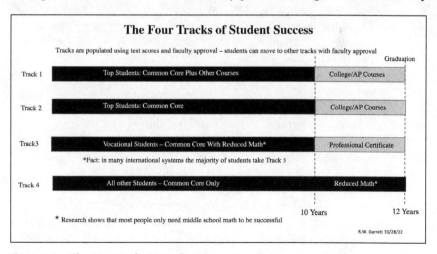

Figure 8.1. The Four Tracks to Student Success

the brightest students are assigned to track 1. One of the issues discussed in chapter 3 is to establish consequences. One of the consequences of a poor test score is a lower track. School administrators must stand their ground regarding consequences, as was pointed out in chapter 3, and students need to learn to deal with setbacks as they work to build confidence and character.

What is a Common Core? This expression can light fires in some states where it is believed that using the government-provided Common Core was butting into the rights of the states. Call it what you may, but someone, some group must lay out what needs to be learned during each semester for every grade from K to 12. It will be called the Common Core in this book. Each track has the responsibility to complete the Common Core in the allotted times: 10 years for tracks 1, 2, and 3; 12 years for track 4.

Here is a discussion of each track:

Track 1: This track is for the best and the brightest. On track 1 the students not only follow the Common Core, but they also take additional courses as well. In years 11 and 12 they are basically in college taking college level courses. These courses are free, so they are going to avoid 2 years at a university as they work toward their bachelor's degree. This is no different from the AP (Advanced Placement) courses they currently take in their later years of high school. It will be very gratifying to be able to complete their university degree in about 2 years.

Track 2: This track is identical to track 1, but the students only focus on the Common Core until the end of year 10. From then on, it's identical to track 1.

Track 3: This is the career/vocational path. In the better international systems, many students follow this path. In the advanced nations, the majority of the students do NOT move on to a university degree. They opt for a career in technology, tool and die making, and so forth since most of the developed nations have very good jobs for these people.

Unfortunately, such job programs here in the U.S. are just developing and the program has a long way to go. Track 3 is as rigorous as track 2 except for mathematics. Research has found that most high school graduates never need math skills beyond what they learned in middle school. Consequently, the math requirement for track 3 is to master middle school math. This change will make this track much more appealing to many U.S. students.

The objective of this track is not a high school diploma but a certificate that certifies that the student is competent in the skill or trade they are pursuing. The possible trades, skill sets, and so forth are so diverse the students need to be exposed to some of the possibilities before entering high school. The way to do this is to organize an eighth-grade program that will present to the students a wide range of possibilities for the earning of certificates of competence.

In Belgium, one of the areas of certification is the use of gas chromatograph, a machine that analyzes the content of a sample, thereby describing the component chemicals that are present in the submitted sample. This job puts the student in a laboratory where they become the "go to" guy for operating this complex machine. Sounds like a pretty good job.

> *Track 4:* This is the track for all other students. It is not a dumping ground and will not be seen as such if it is rigorous and well taught. This track also has a reduced math requirement. When completed, the students should have a solid grasp of the Common Core curriculum.

HOW MUCH MATH DOES AN
AVERAGE PERSON NEED?

Why are average people required to take math well beyond what they will ever need? Here are thoughts on math usage.

> As it turns out, less than a quarter of U.S. workers report using math any more complicated than basic fractions and percentages during the course of their jobs. The graphs (see figures 8.2 and 8.3) are based on survey data compiled by Northeastern University sociologist Michael Handel. Handel surveyed about 2,300 workers first from 2004 through 2006, then again between 2007 and 2009.
>
> The catchall category of "any more advanced" math includes algebra through calculus. And as you can see, most workers aren't doing a whole lot of high-level computations.[1]

You might be surprised by who's doing the most advanced math day-to-day. It's not white-collar workers. Rather, it's high-skill blue-collar workers, shown in dark blue on the graph below. Before you glance over it, here's a breakdown of jobs categories:

- Upper-level white collar (e.g., management, technical, and professional occupations)
- Lower-level white collar (e.g., clerical and sales workers)
- Upper-level blue collar (e.g., craft and repair workers like skilled construction trades and mechanics)
- Lower-level blue collar (e.g., factory workers and truck drivers)

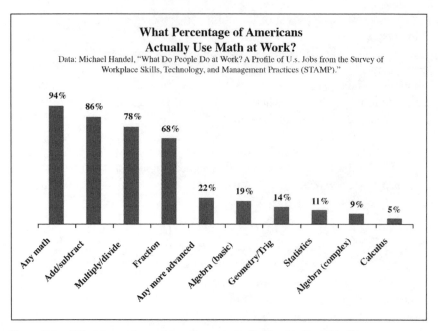

Figure 8.2. What Percentage of Americans Actually Use Math at Work?

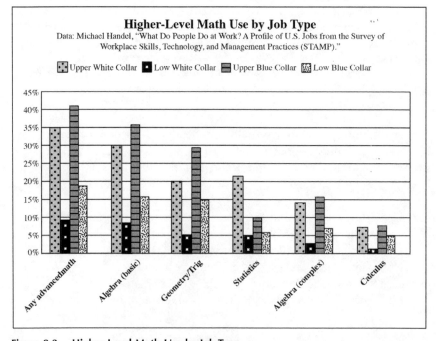

Figure 8.3. Higher-Level Math Use by Job Type

WHAT IS MIDDLE SCHOOL MATH?

Grades 6, 7, and 8 make up middle school. What math courses are taught in "middle school math?" Because math can be difficult to understand, a middle school math sequence is defined below to give the reader an idea of the course content. This sequence comes from Fusion Schools, a private system of 80 campuses scattered throughout America. Table 8.1 shows the four-course sequence.[2]

COURSE DESCRIPTIONS

Math Course 1 is the first of two courses in an integrated middle school mathematics sequence designed to prepare students for Pre-Algebra. The content present in the course covers five main areas of mathematics: ratios and proportional reasoning, the number system, expressions and equations, geometry, and statistics.

Students begin to extend their knowledge of arithmetic with whole numbers to numbers including fractions and decimals. They also explore the fundamental aspects of algebra involving the concept of a variable and solving one-step equations, especially in the context of real-world applications.

In Math Course 2, students work more closely with fractions in this course as they begin to develop an understanding of all operations with rational numbers extending into more complex linear equations. This broadens their view of the number system and allows for connections to previous courses. There is a heavy emphasis on real-world applications in relation to percent, scale drawings, and area/volume concepts.

Pre-Algebra prepares students for Algebra 1. The course covers five main areas of mathematics: the number system, expressions and equations, functions, geometry, and statistics and probability. Students extend their fundamental knowledge of algebraic concepts to include the concept of a function, and to extrapolate to make predictions.

Algebra 1. Algebra 1 is a foundational math course that focuses both on computational competency and conceptual understanding with application. Topics

Table 8.1. Middle School Math Curriculum

Middle School Match Curriculum
Math Course 1 - 2 semesters
Math Course 2 - 2 semesters
Pre-Algebra - 2 semesters
Algebra 1 - 2 semesters

include solving, graphing, and describing diverse equations, linear equations and inequalities, systems of equations, exponential functions and polynomial functions and data analysis.

IN SUMMARY

This chapter is advocating for a school system with a tracked design. It acknowledges that the many words written about tracked versus no-tracks do not make it clear as to which is the most advantageous. It is also acknowledged that there may be resistance in the community to stratifying training by ability levels, but by doing so, it is hoped that this design will lead to better individual learning. Hopefully having mobility from track to track and high-quality teaching on every track, this division of students will be found acceptable.

This chapter also advocates for a reduced math program for two of the tracks: track 3, the professional trades track and track 4, the Common Core only track. The evidence presented shows there is very little value in math training beyond middle school math for many of our citizens. There is a math need in our "blue collar" sector, and if the described math training is not adequate, the needed math will be covered in years 11 and 12.

NOTES

1. Weissmann, Jordan, "Here's How Little Math Americans Actually Use at Work," *The Atlantic*, April 24, 2013, https://www.theatlantic.com/business/archive/2013/04/heres-how-little-math-americans-actually-use-at-work/275260/

2. "Middle and High School Math Classes at Fusion Academy," Fusion Academy, https://www.fusionacademy.com/curriculum/math-classes/

Chapter 9

Learning to Read

The most fundamental of all academic skills is reading. A child learns to read from the time they enter school until the end of the third grade, then uses this skill to learn for the rest of their lives.

A child learns to read from the time they enter school until the end of the third grade, then uses this skill to learn for the rest of their lives.

As discussed in chapter 2, many high school graduates have not mastered reading. In literacy, 25% (49 million) have the reading skills of a 10-year-old, placing America 12th among 29 nations as measured by the Program for the International Assessment of Adult Competencies (PIAAC). This dismal level of verbal competence worsened from 20% in the program's previous 2012 study. In other words, reading skills are getting worse! How can a high school student who cannot read be granted a diploma?

In chapter 2, the focus was on performance measures and America's generally mediocre performance in most areas. These results are disappointing; America should do much better.

Social promotion is the movement of a student from one grade to the next even though the student has not met the academic requirements for promotion. An argument is made that retaining the student will damage their self-esteem. They will feel like a failure, and this feeling will have a major impact on their lives.

When it comes to feeling like a failure, how are they going to feel if they go through the rest of their lives unable to read beyond the level of a 10-year-old child? This lack of skill will be a major impediment to entering and graduating from college and will most likely impact them in most good jobs.

Are they forever doomed? What does the research say?

One in six children who are not reading proficiently in third grade do not graduate from high school on time, a rate four times greater than that for proficient readers.

The rates are highest for the low, below-basic readers: 23% of these children drop out or fail to finish high school on time, compared to 9% of children with basic reading skills and 4% of proficient readers.

The below-basic readers account for a third of the sample but three-fifths of the students who do not graduate.

Overall, 22% of children who have lived in poverty do not graduate from high school, compared to 6% of those who have never been poor. This rises to 32% for students spending more than half of the survey time in poverty.

For children who were poor for at least a year and were not reading proficiently in third grade, the proportion of those who don't finish school rose to 26%. The rate was highest for poor black and Hispanic students, at 31% and 33% respectively. Even so the majority of students who fail to graduate are white.

Even among poor children who were proficient readers in third grade, 11% still didn't finish high school. That compares to 9% of subpar third graders who were never poor.

Among children who never lived in poverty, all but 2% of the best third grade readers graduated from high school on time.

Poverty compounds the problem: Students who have lived in poverty are three times more likely to drop out or fail to graduate on time than their more affluent peers; if they read poorly, too, the rate is six times greater than that for all proficient readers, the study found. For black and Latino students, the combined effect of poverty and poor third-grade reading skills makes the rate eight times greater.

We will never close the achievement gap, we will never solve our dropout crisis, we will never break the cycle of poverty that afflicts so many children if we don't make sure that all our students learn to read," said Ralph Smith, executive vice president of the Annie E. Casey Foundation, which commissioned the report.[1]

How can anyone who works in education approve of social promotion?

DATA FROM OHIO

The state of Ohio was determined to keep children from moving into the fourth grade who could not read at the required level. State law required schools to hold back these children. They worked under this law for about a decade; their goal was to eliminate social promotion. The "falling behind" students received special training aimed at improving reading proficiency.

Common sense and some evidence of improved reading skills aside, the Ohio state legislature tossed aside the reading requirement. The schools vowed to continue with the reading improvement program even though it was no longer the law. Look at the graph in figure 9.1.[2]

These are the larger cities in Ohio. The taller bars show the proportion of third graders that were promoted into grade four; the shorter bars show

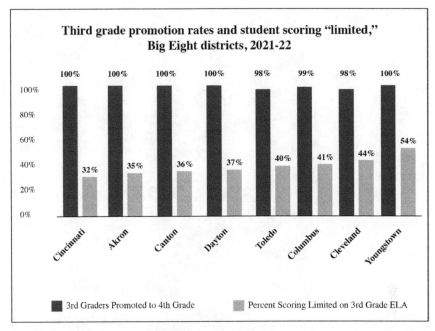

Figure 9.1. Third-Grade Promotion Rates and Students Scoring "Limited," Big Eight Districts 2021–2022

the percentage of the students who did not pass the reading assessment exam. These are the children who should have been held back. For example, Youngstown promoted all third graders while 54% of them were not properly prepared. Only a tiny number in three of the cities (those with less than 100% advancement numbers) were held back. This is a picture of social promotion at its worst.

Figure 9.2 shows test score data from the National Center for Educational Progress (NAEP) for public school students who were tested in the winter of their fourth year, soon after being promoted to the fourth grade. The bars show reading scores as a percentage of all students taking the test for the nation for the years 1992 to 2022. In other words, look at the first horizontal bar for the year 2022; 39% of all test takers scores were in the "Below Basic" level. Having no data on students who were held back, with 39% failing the reading exam, it is a safe assumption that essentially all students were advanced.

Assume a "below-basic" score is a failing score. Consequently, 37% of the third graders (the average for all years shown) should have been "held back" but weren't. Nationally this is in the ballpark of 2.2 million students each year.

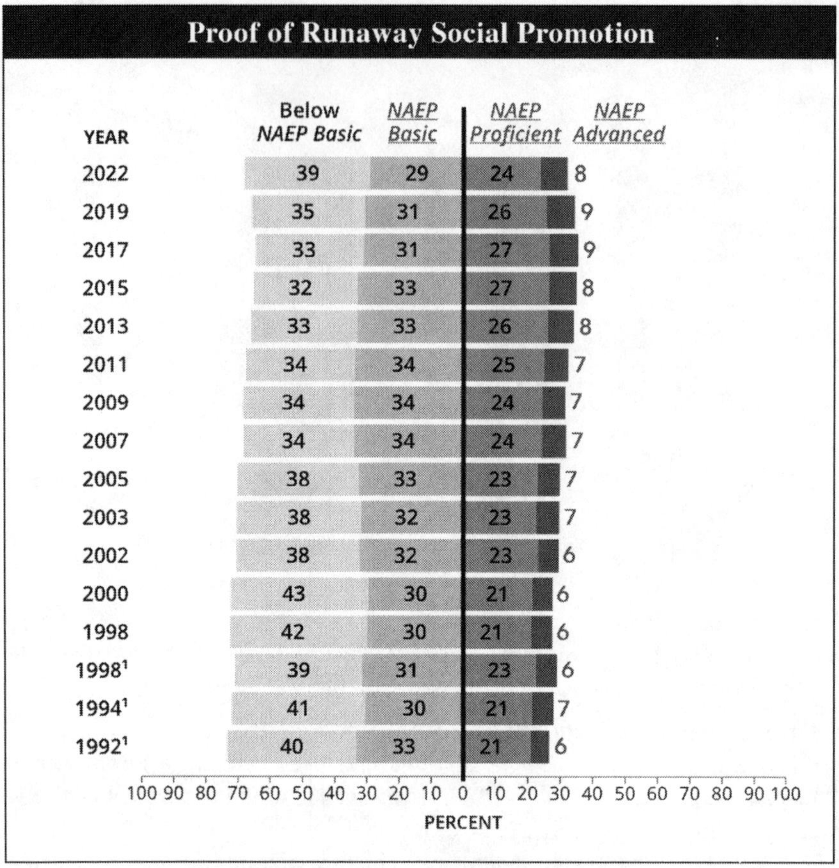

Proof of Runaway Social Promotion

YEAR	Below NAEP Basic	*NAEP Basic*	*NAEP Proficient*	*NAEP Advanced*
2022	39	29	24	8
2019	35	31	26	9
2017	33	31	27	9
2015	32	33	27	8
2013	33	33	26	8
2011	34	34	25	7
2009	34	34	24	7
2007	34	34	24	7
2005	38	33	23	7
2003	38	32	23	7
2002	38	32	23	6
2000	43	30	21	6
1998	42	30	21	6
1998[1]	39	31	23	6
1994[1]	41	30	21	7
1992[1]	40	33	21	6

100 90 80 70 60 50 40 30 20 10 0 10 20 30 40 50 60 70 80 90 100

PERCENT

Figure 9.2.   NAEP Reading Test Scores by Achievement Level

Fourth graders are tested in the winter of the year, so they have been taking reading for a few months at the fourth-grade level. Because the students are already in the fourth grade, they carried with them their reading skills. All these children got promoted into the fourth grade; all were socially promoted! The first stack of bars in the above graph, the below "NAEP Basic" score, shows a social promotion rate in the 37% range. It is no wonder America's students have low scores, as many of them never learned how to read at a suitable level.

This explains one of the more disappointing test results presented in chapter 2. The tests say 25% of American high school graduates have the reading ability of a 10-year-old child; this is about 49 million people. This chapter shows how our schools are the feeder system for this population adding about 2.2 million poor readers every year.

Why are students being pushed forward so forcefully? There seems to be a strong desire to "get rid of these kids"; teachers do not want to have to deal with them for another year. Additionally, these students are problematic for the school in that they require extra expense. Combine this with the feelings of the parents who don't want their child held back and this leads to large numbers of children who should have been held back but weren't. What is the right thing to do? The correct action is to hold them back and develop an appropriate level of reading skills. Ideally, the diagnosis and corrective action would have happened in earlier years so the student would not fail the test at the end of the third grade.

CAN EVERY STUDENT LEARN TO READ?

What does science say about reading? Given the proper amount of time and energy, can all children learn to read? Here are thoughts on this question.

Good readers are phonemically aware, understand the alphabetic principle, apply these skills in a rapid and fluent manner, possess strong vocabularies and syntactical and grammatical skills, and relate reading to their own experiences.

Difficulties in any of these areas can impede reading development. Further, learning to read begins far before children enter formal schooling. Children who have stimulating literacy experiences from birth onward have an edge in vocabulary development, understanding the goals of reading, and developing an awareness of print and literacy concepts.

Conversely, the children who are most at risk for reading failure enter kindergarten and the elementary grades without these early experiences. Frequently, many poor readers have not consistently engaged in the language play that develops an awareness of sound structure and language patterns. They have limited exposure to bedtime and lap time reading.

In short, children raised in poverty, those with limited proficiency in English, those from homes where the parents' reading levels and practices are low, and those with speech, language, and hearing handicaps are at increased risk of reading failure.

However, many children with robust oral language experience, average to above average intelligence, and frequent early interactions with literacy activities also have difficulties learning to read. Why?

Programmatic longitudinal research, including research supported by NICHD, clearly indicates that deficits in the development of phoneme awareness skills not only predict difficulties learning to read, but they also have a negative effect on reading acquisition. Whereas phoneme awareness is necessary for adequate reading development, it is not sufficient. Children must also develop phonics concepts and apply these skills fluently in text.

Although substantial research supports the importance of phoneme awareness, phonics, and the development of speed and automaticity in reading, we
know less about how children develop reading comprehension strategies and
semantic and syntactic knowledge. Given that some children with well-developed decoding and word-recognition abilities have difficulties understanding
what they read, more research in reading comprehension is crucial.[3]

This supports, as do thousands of other articles, the urgency to *START EARLY*
with reading.

If a child with low reading skills is promoted anyway, can they "catch up"?
As you will see, the answer is "yes," but it requires an intensive effort, an
effort that most children will never receive. Here is commentary from reading experts:

As I travel across the country speaking to groups of parents about reading difficulties, I often say "beware of the developmental lag excuse." I have several
reasons for saying this. First, I have listened to parent after parent tell me about
feeling there was a problem early on yet being persuaded to discount their intu-
ition and wait to seek help for their child.

Later, when they learned time was of the essence in developing reading skills,
the parents regretted the lost months or years. Second, research shows that the
crucial window of opportunity to deliver help is during the first couple of years
of school. So, if your child is having trouble learning to read, the *best approach
is to take immediate action*.

Knowing how soon to act can be easy if you are informed about important
conclusions from recent research. Reading researchers tell us the ideal window
of opportunity for addressing reading difficulties is during kindergarten and first
grade. *The National Institutes of Health says that 95% of poor readers can be
brought up to grade level if they receive effective help early*.

While it is still possible to help an older child with reading, those beyond
third grade require much more intensive help. The longer you wait to get help
for a child with reading difficulties, the harder it will be for the child to catch up.

The three key research conclusions that support seeking help early are:

- 90% of children with reading difficulties will achieve grade level in reading if they receive help by the first grade
- 75% of children whose help is delayed to age nine or later continue to
  struggle throughout their school careers.
- If help is given in fourth grade, rather than in late kindergarten, it takes
  four times as long to improve the same skills by the same amount.

Parents who understand these research conclusions realize they cannot afford
to waste valuable time trying to figure out if there really is a problem or waiting
for the problem to cure itself.[4]

If a child is promoted with inadequate reading skills, can they catch up later? As was stated above, the answer is yes but it is highly unlikely. Keep in mind that the reading material advances in complexity as the grades go by. This compounds the problem. Here are the three fundamental points:

1. 90% of children with reading difficulties will achieve grade level in reading if they receive help by the first grade
2. 75% of children whose help is delayed to age nine or later continue to struggle throughout their school careers.
3. If help is given in fourth grade, rather than in late kindergarten, it takes four times as long to improve the same skills by the same amount.

Foundational skills such as reading must be developed before the first grade, and they must be corrected before the first grade. Therefore, this book recommends formal school beginning at the age of 3. At this age teachers get a running start to focus on children who are having trouble.

Can students with a low IQ or learning disabilities learn to read? The answer is yes, but some/most do not develop strong skills. Consider this expert commentary:

> The findings of a pioneering four-year educational study offer hope for thousands of children identified with intellectual disability or low IQ who have very little, if any, reading ability. The study by researchers at Southern Methodist University, Dallas, is the first large-scale longitudinal study of its kind to demonstrate the reading potential of students with intellectual disability or low IQ, said lead author Jill H. Allor, principal investigator of the study, which was funded by the U.S. Department of Education.
>
> The researchers found that students with intellectual disability who participated in four years of persistent, specialized instruction successfully learned to read at a first-grade level or higher.[5]

Combining all this material leads to the conclusion that essentially all students can learn to read. The strategy is to: (1) Start as early as possible, ideally around ages 1–2 to acquaint children with books and to begin to let them experience the magic of the marvelous things that come from books; and (2) Pour on the resources if a child is struggling. This is obviously a financial drain on the school district, but that is one of the magjor needed reforms to the U.S. educational system.

This is analogous to trying to teach an adult a new foreign language. This is tough to do; it is possible but very demanding.

A PROCESS FOR DETERMINING WHICH STUDENTS GET PROMOTED TO THE FOURTH GRADE

If at the end of the second grade, a student's reading skills are not developing well enough, the parent(s) will be informed that their student is a candidate to be held back at the end of their third grade. This is an early warning that will hopefully activate reading intervention over the summer to attempt move the child back on schedule so they will be able to be promoted to the fourth grade.

This intervention, by reading experts, parents, and volunteers will work throughout the third year to raise the skills up to the needed level. If, at the end of the third grade, the skills are not yet in place, the summer between the third and fourth grades is the final opportunity for improvement. At the end of the summer, if the student's reading skills are still below the required level, they will repeat the third grade.

NOTES

1. No author listed, "Students Who Don't Read Well in Third Grade Are More Likely to Drop Out or Fail to Finish High School," *Annie E Casey Foundation,* April 8, 2011. The quotations used here are in this article but not in the format or the sequence presented. https://www.aeci.org/blog/poverty-puts-struggling-readers-in-double-jeopardy-minorities-most-at-risk

2. Churchill, Aaron, "'Social Promotion' Returns Without State Reading Requirement," The Thomas Fordham Institute, October 11, 2022, https://fordhaminstitute.org/ohio/commentary/social-promotion-returns-without-state-reading-requirement

3. Lyon, G. Reid, "Why Some Children Have Difficulties Learning to Read," *Reading Rockets,* Excerpted from: Lyon, G. R. (January/February 2000). *Why reading is not a natural process. LDA Newsbriefs.* Learning Disabilities Association of America, https://www.readingrockets.org/article/why-some-children-have-difficulties-learning-read

4. Hall, Susan, "Is It a Reading Disorder or Developmental Lag?," *Reading Rockets,* no date given, https://www.readingrockets.org/article/it-reading-disorder-or-developmental-lag

5. "Low IQ Students Learn to Read at 1st-grade Level After Persistent, Intensive Instruction," *Reading Rockets,* May 21, 2014, https://www.readingrockets.org/news/low-iq-students-learn-read-1st-grade-level-after-persistent-intensive-instruction

Chapter 10

When Should Formal Education Begin?

Does beginning a child's formal education at 3 years old make sense? Their brains are like sponges that soak up way more than we realize. It is a prime period of brain development when the brain needs lots of exercise to develop fully and properly.

Thus, one of the primary objectives of 3-year-old children to be in school is to guarantee they receive the proper amount of brain stimulation. This is especially true for students from lower socio-economic levels who may not receive the necessary brain stimulation at home.

Children reared in middle- and upper-class families receive lots of stimulation. Their parents read to them and introduce them the joys of books. They go on vacations and see all manner of interesting things. They go to the zoo, to children's museums, and on and on. Parents enroll their children in early education classes as soon as possible, many beginning at 3 years old.

Unfortunately, children from less affluent families are not so lucky. Their parents struggle to provide enough income to keep the family housed and fed, they work several jobs, and a family vacation is just a dream. These are the children who may not receive anywhere near the brain stimulation that will allow for brain development approaching their genetic potential. They need guaranteed stimulation from sources outside of their families. These are the kids who are candidates for a formal program beginning at 3 years old.

What kinds of things can a 3-year-old learn? Here is a list of things a 3-year-old should know and demonstrate before turning 4.

Emotional Awareness

At this age, children are not only becoming more aware of their own emotions, but also that of others.

For example, around three years of age, children will develop empathy for others, being more aware of others' feelings. Additionally, children will start to show affection for others, in ways such as hugging a friend without being asked to do so.

Because your toddler is becoming more aware of his/her feelings, you can start to have him/her start identifying those feelings. For example, encourage him/her to say things like, "I'm happy," or, "I'm sad," and explain why s/he feels that way.

Moreover, as their imaginations expand and their social skills develop, three-year-olds will also stray from playing independently and begin playing with other children. Often, this will include group games and real-life games such as "house" or "school."

Cognitive Skills

Your child's cognitive skills will grow exponentially as he or she grows! For this reason, it's important you are aware of the things s/he should know at this age. Following are some academic milestones a three-year-old should be able to accomplish.

- Say name and age
- Answer simple questions
- Recite the alphabet
- Identify basic shapes and colors
- Tell stories
- Count (to at least 10)
- Know about 300–500 words as well as understand many others
- Understand the difference and similarity between things and sort them accordingly
- Complete age-appropriate puzzles
- Understand time (morning, night, days of the week)
- Follow three-step instructions, such as, "Brush your teeth, put your pajamas on, and get into bed."
- Use basic grammar rules. Children may still mess up words that are exceptions to basic grammar rules, such as saying "mouses" instead of "mice."
- Ask a lot of questions, such as "why?" Be sure to be patient with them and encourage their curiosity.

Furthermore, by the time a child turns three, s/he should be speaking in full sentences of at least six words or more. By the age of four, s/he should be able to speak in complete sentences. Your little one will grow a lot in the next year![1]

This is an impressive list and offers a lot for a child to be taught who is in a class for 3-year-olds. These are all worthwhile items that will benefit the child and its parents.

The Buffett Early Childhood Institute at the University of Nebraska suggests the following:

Ninety percent.

That's the giant part of a child's brain formed by the time she blows out the candles on her sixth birthday cake.

Ninety percent. Those are the first two words that pop into Sam Meisels's head when the founding executive director of the Buffett Early Childhood Institute at the University of Nebraska is quizzed by a stranger.

Ninety percent is our starting point today, as we consider a basic but key question: Why does quality early childhood education matter, anyway?

In 2020, most Nebraskans tell us in surveys that early childhood education is important to them. To parents, especially, the need for help is obvious: Roughly 75% of all young Nebraska children grow up in homes where all parents work.

But what we may lack is a statewide understanding of just how crucial high-quality early childhood education is, and why.

In the past half-century, researchers have learned stunning things about how and how quickly the brain develops—science revolutionizing how we view small children and learning. Experts have done decades-long studies on early childhood programs—work suggesting that a toddler's experiences in early care and education can alter the trajectory of his life.

Not so long ago, we viewed young children as blank slates who didn't need to learn much before entering Kindergarten. *Now we know that stimulating brain growth long before Kindergarten can have a massive impact on her future education, her future earnings, and even her future health.* [italics added]

The shift in thinking began when we started today: 90 percent of a child's brain is formed by the time he turns 6.

Starting the moment you are born, a million neural connections form *each second* in all parts of the brain, says Dr. Jack Shonkoff, director of Harvard University's Center on the Developing Child. That insanely rapid early brain growth builds "the foundation of who we will become as people."

The growth of new connections slows rapidly before puberty. Rewiring existing connections also gets tougher with each passing year. That's why it is much easier to learn a new language at age 7 than age 77.

"It's more efficient, both biologically and economically, to get things right the first time than to try to fix them later," Meisels says. So how do we get things right the first time? There are many ways. High-quality early childhood education can happen in a home, at a school, or an early childhood center. But no matter how it is delivered, a mountain of research shows that good early education can change the lives of young children—especially young children growing up in poverty.[2]

Does Early Education "Pay Off"?

There's a bizarre-seeming paradox sitting at the heart of research into early childhood education. On the one hand, a sizable body of research suggests that kids who go through intensive education at the ages of 3 and 4 don't really come out ahead in terms of academic abilities. By kindergarten, much of their advantage has receded, and by second grade researchers typically can't detect it at all.

On the other hand, an equally substantive body of research suggesting that early childhood education produces a profound, lifelong advantage. Kids who enter intensive preschool programs are less likely to be arrested, more likely to graduate, and less likely to struggle with substance abuse as adults. One study with a follow-up when the students were in their mid-30s found that they were more likely to have eventually attended and completed college.

Why Might Early Learning Results Fade?

Here is a quote of one sentence from the above material. "On the one hand, there's a sizable body of research suggesting that kids who go through intensive education at the ages of 3 and 4 don't really come out ahead in terms of academic abilities. By kindergarten much of their advantage has receded, and by second grade researchers typically can't detect it at all." The way this sentence is presented it seems fruitless to expend the energy early on if it washes out. Look at this from another perspective; a tie isn't all that bad. If they are as capable as other second and third graders that is an accomplishment. They aren't behind!

An Indianapolis kindergarten teacher has a class of 26 kids. Nine of these kids have already been in earlier schooling, like Pre-K, and have well-developed print concepts. The other 17 have no print concepts. It is though they have never touched a book. They can't distinguish the front from the back, and they don't know about pages.

How should the teacher handle this? She has two choices:

1. Try to spend time with each group.
2. Abandon the children with the better developed skill set and bring the balance of the class to a skill set necessary to enter the first grade.

She selects option 2. She does not feel responsible for sending children forward with inadequate reading skills. She doesn't have time for both options.

An alternative is to provide two tracks for several years. One track is for Pre-K readers who are well prepared to advance their skills. The other track is for the 17 students who were behind at the beginning of kindergarten. Unfortunately, the school she is in does not track students.

TEACH GOOD HABITS IN SCHOOL

The Oaks Academy of Indianapolis is a private school that is ranked in the top 20 of Indiana private schools. It is a Pre-K to grade 8 school with approximately 1,151 students in all nine grades. By policy, 40% of the students are black. Their state assessment scores are among the best in the state. To mold good behavior, they phase in habits that go all the way to middle school. Below is their statement on their philosophy and a list of their habits. (This is a religious school and contains one second grade habit on reverence; not wanting to misrepresent their school, it is left in the list.)

> The necessity of forming habits is an integral part of [our] philosophy as they aid one in functioning in relationships. These are not tacked onto one's life as another feat to be mastered in a performance culture, but are used as valuable tools in the intellectual, spiritual, and physical development in relationship to oneself, God, and others.
>
> Maryellen St. Cyr, *When Children Love to Learn*

The habits are listed in the order that they are added at each grade level. All these habits are promoted throughout the school at all grade levels, but certain habits are a focus at each grade level. The habits are cumulative, and middle school students are responsible for all the habits on the list.

Beginning in Pre-K

Habit of Attention: The habit of attention requires that one fix mind/body steadily on the matter at hand.

Habit of Obedience: Obedience is demonstrated by responding immediately and completely to authority, as well as accepting consequences willingly.

Habit of Respect: Showing respect involves using good manners and self-control in words and actions.

Habit of Responsibility: Responsibility is shown when care is given to personal belongings and school property, and tasks are completed.

Added in 2nd Grade

Habit of Reverence: Reverence is demonstrated by one's awe and respect for things of God.

Habit of Reflection: The habit of reflection requires purposeful thinking and contemplation about the matter at hand.

Habit of Thoroughness: Thoroughness involves completing whatever task is at hand to the very best of one's ability, leaving nothing undone.

Habit of Punctuality: To be punctual one's obligations must be met in a timely manner.

Added in Middle School

Habit of Service: In serving, one must think of helping others and meeting their needs in a cheerful manner.

Habit of Self-control: To be self-controlled is to have mastery over one's actions and have the ability to delay gratification.

Habit of Integrity: Integrity involves always being honest and allowing one's words and actions to be above reproach, so that one is seen as trustworthy.[3]

This list was presented to point out that young children can begin to learn the Pre-K habits even at their early age. Learning something as simple as "yes sir" or "yes ma'am," "thank you," and so on will carry a child throughout their lives. These are essential noncognitive skills as spelled out in the success equation of chapter 7.

To wrap up, brain development is vitally important to everyone and especially so for low-income children. All children, especially low-income children, need this beginning at age 3, so they do not miss the prime growth area of age 3 and 4. It is already available at age 5 in kindergarten.

NOTES

1. No author listed, "Things a 3-Year-Old Should Know Through Personal Development," *Smaller Scholars, Montessori Academy.*

2. Hansen, Matthew, "Early Childhood Education Matters, the Science Says It Does," The Buffett Early Childhood Institute at the University of Nebraska, November 12, 2020, https://buffettinstitute.nebraska.edu/news-and-events/early-years-matter/early-childhood-education-matters-the-science-says-it-does

3. No author listed, "The Oaks Academy Family Handbook 22.3," *The Oaks Academy,* Indianapolis, IN, page 7, https://www.theoaksacademy.org/wpcontent/uploads/2021/05/Family_Handbook_22.3-2.pdf

Chapter 11

Who's Going to Fix It?

Suppose something has gone wrong in a U.S. company and the board of directors is very concerned. What do they do? They find out who is responsible for the area under review, and they take corrective action. They might fire the person, demote the person, or give them a stern warning. The important thing is they can find the person responsible and hold them accountable.

Is there a single point of responsibility for education within a state? It must be the state school board in combination with the state superintendent of schools. Is the state superintendent responsible for all state schools? See statement below.

> The superintendent, along with the board of education, sets educational policies and guidelines for public and private schools, preschool through grade 12, as well as vocational education. It analyzes the aims, needs and requirements of education and recommends legislation to the General Assembly and governor.[1]

Do all of Illinois's 852 school superintendents report informally to the state superintendent? No, they report to their local school board. What is the responsibility of a school board? See statement below.

> School board members are tasked with an important responsibility: educating nearly 50 million children—almost nine out of every 10 students—who receive their education in public schools. Board members are more than policymakers and administrators; they are advocates for students and their parents and entrusted to engineer a better future.[2]

To whom does the school board report? They are elected by the people and responsible to the people.

There is a serious problem here. Who is accountable? It looks like the responsibility rests with each of the 852 school boards. How are they to be held accountable?

This is a serious problem when it comes to things like striving for excellence and not widening the plate. Since the school boards are elected positions, they do not want to upset their constituents and lose the next election, so they try to placate them to keep them happy. Suppose they try to tighten up grading standards so 47% of the high school seniors no longer carry an "A" average. This will bring serious repercussions from many of the parents.

So, who fixes the problem of a mediocre state school system? Not members of the school or state administrators. They are the ones who have led us into the poor performing system we are currently in, and they seem content with it the way it is. There is no uproar of discontent from this group..

WHAT IS A BETTER WAY?

Follow the accountability model of business. Let the state superintendent/ school board be the go-to persons for problems like the pursuit of excellence, school quality, and the setting and maintenance of high standards. This gets the local school board members "off the hook" when it comes time to tighten up grading. The state superintendent becomes the education czar for the state with the state school board giving them their "marching orders."

Many of the top international educational systems have tight countrywide-school system management responsibility. They set the standards and policy and it is up to the school district to implement the plans. The national education czar is the person to hold accountable when things go wrong. They work with the entire system, including schools of education, to ensure high standards and high quality. They work with the universities feeding teachers into their systems to ensure they are producing the kind of teachers they desire.

WHERE DO AMERICAN CZARS GET THEIR POWER?

The head of the state's public school system holds a powerful position and needs a way to ensure that their plans are accepted and implemented throughout the state. As usual in government management, they have the "power of the purse," if so granted by the state legislature. Look at school funding:

Property taxation and school funding are closely linked in the United States. In 2018–2019, public education revenue totaled $771 billion. Nearly half (47%) came from state governments, slightly less than half (45%) from local government sources, and a modest share (8%) from the federal government. Of the local revenue, about 36% came from property taxes. The remaining 8.9% was generated from other taxes; fees and charges for things like school lunches and athletic events; and contributions from individuals, organizations, or businesses.[3]

This quotation points out that 47% of school funding comes from the state and does not involve property taxes. That's a very large "fiscal lever" that might be used to mandate the pursuit of excellence and elevated standards.

Here is the action step. The legislature gives the state school board fiscal power to control the distribution of funding to each school district. The control gives the state school board discretionary power over certain funds that can be focused on meeting certain state standards. For example, if the district is giving out too many "A's" they lose some funding. Money is the source of power of the education czar.

Who Leads the Charge for Change?

So, who will lead the charge to improve education in each state? It is not going to come from within the public school system. Folks within this system are causing many of the problems. Who has a strong vested interest in quality education? Certainly, state universities and colleges, but they are a collection of entities without a strong connecting link. Look and the people who hire the state's high school graduates, the employers. This is the right place to concentrate "the force for change" that is so badly needed. Each state has a chamber of commerce or its equivalent that should lead reform efforts.

The Business Vested Interest Illustrated

Wisconsin just completed a report titled *Wisconsin 2035, A Vision for Wisconsin's Economic Future*.[4] As they interviewed their constituents there was a consistent theme, "Where are we going to get our future employees?" About 62,000 students graduate from Wisconsin's public schools. Their CCR (college and career readiness percent) is around 34%.

How many students are *not good* candidates for employment in Wisconsin? To get an output of 62,000 students, 88,600 had to be in the system at some point in the past, using Bill Gates's statistic that cites a 30% dropout average. This represents a loss of about 27,000. This is the first piece of the loss. The next piece is the graduates who are not going to be good hires, the students who are not college and career ready, 66% of the graduating class; another 41,000 students. So, 68,000 students are not good candidates for employment. It would be wonderful for business if some of these folks could be molded into better students.

This is not to say that these folks are hanging around on street corners; they end up finding their way into the economy, but at a much lower level than they might have been.

Does looking at the problem this way generate a stronger vested interest? It certainly does. Massachusetts is number one in education and has been for years. If they *were a country*, they would rank in the top 10 in test scores as administered by PISA, the Program for International Assessment.

It all happened because a group of businesspeople, The Massachusetts Business Alliance for Education, completed a comprehensive education study that led to the Massachusetts Reform Act of 1993. See chapter 14 for more about the Massachusetts miracle.

How should the content of this chapter be put into practice? Ideally, each state's chamber of commerce should move to be the "force for change" for education. One obvious way to accomplish this is to create reform commissions that will study how the current schools are functioning and make recommendations for improvement.

A great deal of expertise is needed to bring in all the great systems from around the world and incorporate these practices in the reform. A great place to find this talent is the National Center on Education and the Economy (NCEE) of Washington, DC. They were instrumental in the reform of education in the state of Maryland; a reform that is just beginning.

Is There Payback for a State?

Is there payback for a state if it makes smart investments in education? The answer is a resounding yes. As will be shown in chapter 14, when Maryland spends an additional $5.1 billion per year on education, they reap an annual return of $11.3 billion. This is a payback of $2.20 for every dollar spent.

NOTES

1. "Superintendent of Schools (state executive office)," *Ballotpedia*, no page number, https://ballotpedia.org/Superintendent_of_Schools_(state_executive_office)

2. The National School Board Association (NSBA), About School Board and Local Governance, https://www.nsba.org/about/about-school-board-and-local-governance

3. Kenyon, Daphne, "Public Schools and the Property Tax, A Comparison of Education Funding Models in Three Separate States," The Lincoln Institute of Land Policy, April 12, 2022, https://www.lincolninst.edu/publications/articles/2022-04-public-schools-property-tax-comparison-education-models

4. Kurt Bauer, Pres. and CEO, Wisconsin Manufacturing and Commerce (WMC), 501 E. Washington Ave., Madison, WI 53703–2914.

Chapter 12

The Threat of Lawsuits Weighs Heavy[1]

A persistent thorn in the sides of teachers and administrators is the threat of being sued. This threat warps much of what they do and distorts behavior in many ways. Every touch, every bad grade, every disciplinary action can turn into a lawsuit. This chapter will investigate some of these thorns and hopefully offer some hope as to what needs to be done to change this situation. This topic is beyond the scope of this book, so it is recommended that the states take a deep dive into this issue as they look for relief.

SOME PARENTS ARE EAGER TO FILE SUIT

Principals worry that parents may threaten to sue the school over even minor disagreements between a teacher about their child. They believe this is a way for parents to force the school to agree with their position concerning the child and perhaps to earn several hundred dollars quickly and easily. There are plenty of plaintiffs' attorneys willing to work on a percentage basis; therefore, the parents have nothing to lose. The school district, on the other hand, must bear the costs of attorneys to defend the suit and invest valuable time and money working with their defense counsel instead of education issues.

EXAMPLES OF WARPED BEHAVIOR

One of the persistent causes of distorted behavior is touching a child. Many schools have a policy that forbids teachers and other adult employees to touch a child. They take this quite literally, no pats on the back, no shaking of hands, no hugs, no to a lot of things we humans, especially children, find valuable, even essential. State laws do not forbid touching, but experience teaches educators that there is no such thing as a "safe touch."

Here are a few examples of applications of this policy:

1. A first-grade teacher is fully engaged in teaching when suddenly, a young girl begins to act out while standing in front of the classroom door. The commonsense way to handle this is to lead the child outside and down to the office, but under the no touch policy, the teacher can't even move her from in front of the door. Teacher calls the office and receives this advice; we'll have the janitor waiting outside while you evacuate the children out of the windows. There is a huge block of lost time here. What a silly decision!
2. A fifth-grade teacher comes to school in pigtails. One of her female students grabs one of her pigtails and will not let go. Following the policy, she cannot force her hand loose. The teacher grabs her own hair at a spot between her scalp and the child's hand and lifts the child off the floor. She proceeds to the office with the child dangling from her pigtail.
3. A teacher, while in the hallway, notices a boy putting his finger over the water fountain jet and squirting water over fellow students, the wall, and the floor. The teacher removes his hand from the fountain and walks him to the office. Later the principal admonishes the teacher for touching the child!
4. A child is having a traumatic event and cannot be touched to lead them from the room. The teacher evacuates the room and calls the mother. The children do not return to the classroom until mother comes to take charge of the student.
5. A child is having a fit, throwing things, swearing, and so forth. The teacher is not allowed to touch the student; they are not allowed to force the child out of the room so school could continue. So, the teacher evacuates the room until mother comes and settles the child down. To get school management involved, a teacher must do this three times in one day!
6. One teacher relates the story of a young girl who was on top of a boy pummeling him with her fists. The teacher warned her five times to stop and leave the boy alone, but she paid no attention to her. Finally, the teacher lifted the little girl off the boy and took her to the principal's office. She was the one who got into trouble—the principal criticized the teacher for touching the girl! The little girl was soon back in the classroom with no serious reprimand.[2]

HOW DOES THE THREAT OF LAWSUITS
MODIFY BEHAVIOR?

A recent Harris Interactive survey conducted for the organization Common Good revealed that 82% of teachers and 77% of principals say the current legal climate has changed the way they work. *More than 60% of principals surveyed said they had been threatened with a legal challenge.*

"The current legal atmosphere creates a more cautious approach for me and my district," Dr. Lee Yeager, principal at S&S Middle School in Sadler, Texas, told *Education World*. "We are always considering the legal ramifications of issues with students and staff. The threat of a lawsuit, no matter how frivolous, is something that colors many decisions we make." Mary Smith told *Education World*, "I look at everything from a legal perspective. When I come across new territory in decision making, I imagine myself on the witness stand being cross-examined. I mentally review my answers."

Pat Green has been in education for more than 30 years. During that time, she has watched the world become more litigious. "I've heard folks banter, 'I'm going to call my lawyer, when they dislike a decision I've made, regardless of the nature of the choices, good or poor, they or their child made. It's an easy mantra meant to create an aura of fear." The threat of legal action can easily steal away a principal's focus.

"The real challenge is for administrators to remain focused on moving for-ward while the major drain on energy would have us looking over our shoul-ders," said one principal who chose to remain anonymous. "It is difficult to look forward when your head is pointed backward."

Principal Paul Young has served recently as a mentor to future principals. "I see the legal atmosphere impacting my mentees," Young, principal at West Elementary School in Lancaster, Ohio, told *Education World*. "Sometimes they are afraid to take a stand for fear they will anger someone. They are afraid they'll be sued. Two of them have already been involved in lawsuits, and they are just 30 years old."

Many principals say that, over the last 20 years, the overall atmosphere in schools has changed because of the way schools handle discipline issues. "The threat of lawsuits from parents regarding students, especially students in special education, has changed the way teachers and schools work," said principal Lee Yeager. "At one time, if a student was disruptive or a discipline problem, you could remove the student easily. Today, the process is more involved and the threat of, or fear of, a lawsuit makes principals more tolerant."

The area of teacher performance is another area where administrators today are often a bit more cautious than they were several years ago, added Green. "More items are noted in writing today; more procedures and policies are detailed; timelines are met. Particularly in the personnel arena, folks are careful to ensure that employees' rights are represented, and issues are clearly addressed."[3]

Document, Document

One thing a school must do is document. Once the preliminary work gets started on a potential case, a common practice is to call upon the school to produce the documentation of the proper process to handle this situation. The school must set up an active process of keeping this documentation up to date and ensuring that all staff members know and follow the procedures. Next, review the notes written about the event in question. What happened and what actions were taken by the teacher?

If the action taken is in concert with the documented procedure, the school has a good case, and sometimes this step will stop the suit in its tracks.

If you have all the proper documentation, all is in order, and all decisions were reasonable and prudent, then you have your defenses up for any lawsuit. If all things are otherwise equal, the team with the best documentation wins the case.

DO TEACHERS HAVE QUALIFIED IMMUNITY?

What is "qualified immunity"? Qualified immunity protects the individual when they are performing their duties if they do not violate the rights of individuals they serve. Qualified immunity is provided to many public officials such as policemen, firemen, judges, and so forth. Yes, teachers are also offered this protection. Here is a more formal look at this concept:

> Qualified immunity is a type of legal immunity. "Qualified immunity balances two important interests—the need to hold public officials accountable when they exercise power irresponsibly and the need to shield officials from harassment, distraction, and liability when they perform their duties reasonably."
>
> Specifically, qualified immunity protects a government official from lawsuits alleging that the official violated a plaintiff's rights, only allowing suits where officials violated a "clearly established" statutory or constitutional right.
>
> When determining whether a right was "clearly established," courts consider whether a hypothetical reasonable official would have known that the defendant's conduct violated the plaintiff's rights. Courts conducting this analysis apply the law that was in force at the time of the alleged violation, not the law in effect when the court considers the case.[4]

This sounds like an ideal situation for a teacher or administrator, but that is not always the case. Here are the important qualifying words for this to work in the teacher's favor: "a reasonable official would have known that the defendant's conduct violated the plaintiff's rights." These are constitutional rights, rights that are broadly outlined by the state or federal constitution.

Case Law When Immunity Is Not Granted

A middle school student was involved in an altercation at school with a school staff member. The student, who was forcibly removed from the classroom for misconduct, accused the educator of pulling her hair, pushing, punching, and throwing her out of the classroom.

The court noted the fact-based elements in the student's complaint, holding that, "although the undisputed facts show that defendant's initial decision to seize plaintiff and remove her from the classroom was reasonable, [the student's] allegations of punching, hitting and slamming her to the ground create a genuine issue of material fact." In reaching this conclusion, the *court rejected the immunity defense* of the school official.[5]

One of the fundamental principles of this book is the preservation of instruction time. This case presents a dilemma. Ideally the student would leave the room without incident thereby making this a non-event. But with the arousal of anger on both sides, how does the school force the student if she refuses all offers and demands to stay in the room? Persuasion does not work and all that is left is force.

Can force be applied in a rapid and acceptable way and not violate her rights? If the confrontation is not quickly drawn to a close this will ruin a huge portion of the instruction time because the agitated remaining students cannot quickly return to a learning mental state.

Another Case: A Different Situation

In *Meyers v. Cincinnati Bd. of Education*, the United States Court of Appeals ruled that reckless conduct by an elementary school principal and assistant principal eliminated governmental immunity from claims by parents of a third-grade student who committed suicide after several violent incidents at school. The court ruled that immunity under state law was not available for schools that fail to report child abuse, fail to inform parents about prior threats, fail to discipline the student assailants, and fail to call 911 after a serious assault.

One thing is clear from legal research: in order to retain immunity, a school must follow the proper procedures. This case illustrates the need to do the right thing and not be undisciplined about process.

There are many more case examples, but these two make the point. Yes, teachers have qualified immunity but only if they follow good process and do not violate students' rights.

Expulsion and Rights to Education

Expulsion should be considered in certain situations. Is public education a right and is expulsion violating this right? Generally, the area of public education is a matter for the states to address; it is not an enumerated right in the U.S. Constitution. Every child has the right to free public education but when their actions violate other students' rights, the legal right of education for the offending student falls away. Why is yelling out "FIRE" in a crowded theater not an allowed application of the First Amendment? Because it violates the rights of others in a malicious way.

Likewise, if a disruptive student's unruly behavior is wasting large portions of the 220 minutes of instruction time, they are depriving their classmates of their education. The offending student is still legally eligible for an education but only when their behavior does not deprive other students of theirs.

So, if an expelled student undergoes behavior training and modifies their conduct to not be offensive to fellow students or teachers, they may be readmitted. This admission may be as much as a year later if that is what is necessary to slot them into a class they are qualified to take.

Why Do Schools Seek to Settle Potential Lawsuits?

Once a plaintiff files documentation that they are going to sue a school, school districts are prone to try to reach a settlement quickly rather than submit their case to a jury. Here is an example of why they do not want to face a jury.

> Attorneys Richard Barone and Amelia Steelhead successfully obtained a $1,625,000 verdict in Alhambra (CA) after their client Damian was stabbed as he was leaving school. Damian's friend was involved in a failed conflict resolution at school that day and the two students were attacked by gang members when they left school that same day. The attorneys at Rose, Klein & Marias fought hard through multiple defense motions and when no sufficient settlement offers were extended, Mr. Barone and Ms. Steelhead tried the case on behalf of Damian.
>
> After a three-week trial, the jury returned a verdict of $1,625,000 against the school district, assigning 85% of responsibility to the school for failing to adequately resolve the conflict and safely dismiss the students.[6]

On the face of it, just looking at the above words, this seems like an *absurd outcome*. What in the world would the school have needed to do to properly resolve this conflict earlier in the day? If, after they got the students to "make up" or whatever the conclusion of the conflict was, how are they to be held responsible for a gang stabbing after school?

Perhaps the school needs something like this to absolve them of any responsibility:

> I, Johnnie Doe, hereby pledge that Teddy Smith and I have resolved our conflict and the school is no longer to be held responsible for anything that happens between us. More specifically, I pledge to not meet with Teddy Smith and stab him after school today. (High sarcasm)

They Sit on Juries

For whatever reason, there seems to be a desire to punish and demean teachers. Juries are made up with folks like those in the above case who are empaneled and rule on schools! In this case they delivered a mighty blow to an innocent party. Hopefully, this judgment was appealed and the fine lowered, but that involves even more legal expenses by the school district. There is no magic source of money; it all comes from us, the taxpayers.

REMEDIES TO AVOID TRIAL

This topic is beyond the abilities of the author, but a few ideas will be submitted that were derived from consultation with an experienced education law attorney. This section is written for lay readers. Generally, recommendations on the topic of remedies should be determined by school officials, attorneys, and judges.

The current national tendency to focus on individuals and their rights leads to this outcome:

> *Schools Often Sacrifice the Many for the Few*
> *The Time Has Come to Sacrifice the Few for the Many*

School Policy/Process Manual

What are the consequences if a student is not properly dressed? Will they be told they cannot wear "that outfit" again and sent back to class or will they be sent home to change into something that meets code?

This expands into a long list of policies and processes. The school needs to ensure the parents read and understand these processes. Ideally, they send the material home with the students and the parents return a pledge saying they understand and will follow the procedures as written. This pledge should protect the school from some legal actions. If parents do not return the pledge, they weaken their ability to sue.

EXPULSIONS

This book documents the sorry nature of the country's discipline problems and its impact on learning and teachers. Drastic corrective action is in order and one of these actions is expulsion. The student must be given every opportunity to control themselves, but if these attempts fail, expulsion should be considered. Teachers are leaving the profession because of discipline issues; college students are not considering teaching because of stories and experiences in classrooms; other students are being deprived of instruction time.

By state law, every student has the right to 12 years of free education. This applies to disruptive students as well as all others. However, if through their actions, the disruptive students are depriving the balance of the class of their constitutional rights, the protections of the disruptive student "fall away." To establish how the actions of the "bad apple" affect the classroom, documentation of number of incidents, nature of the incidents, and duration of incidents, and so forth must be created.

The duration of the expulsion should be long enough for the student to develop an appreciation of their negative impact and establish the needed self-control to return to class. It would be likely that this will take some time, and if the student "shapes up" they will be allowed to return to school and pick up where they left off. This is probably a year later. If they never gain control of themselves, they never return to school.

This is harsh, but it avoids the loss of knowledge for the balance of the class as they are deprived learning time. In addition, we have taken action that will "allow the teacher to do their job," producing a big boost to morale. To keep teachers in the classrooms, every effort must be made to keep them happy.

AVOIDING TRIALS

Trials are expensive and risky, and to be avoided if possible. It is recommended that states consider alternative dispute resolution (ADR) to avoid trial. ADR relies on mediation or arbitration, instead of a trial, to resolve disputes. This is common practice in many civil family law situations such as divorces. It is either a legislated act or cooperatively put into practice in cases where both parties agree to use it.

For example, the state legislature could create an act that says: all cases involving a teacher, or any other school official, touching a child without sexual overtones or significant physical injury must be resolved by ADR. This act would expand to include other kinds of disagreements as well. If the legislature is not inclined to codify this type of case distinctions for the use of ADR into law, it may be possible to establish it through cooperative agreements between parties. This may be a way to lessen the risks and impact of legal actions against schools and teachers.

This is an area that needs serious attention by state legislatures because of the negative impact it is having on the daily running of a school. Teachers and administrators cannot remain effective if they must constantly be looking over their shoulders for a possible lawsuit.

NOTES

1. What does it take to file a lawsuit? A filing fee and some paperwork. The Indiana filing fee is in the range of $150 to $175. That's it, that's it to file. You can sue anyone about anything, and schools and teachers are frequent targets.

2. Garrett, Richard, taken from Teacher meeting #1, an informal sit-down with several teachers after school. March 19, 2021.

3. Hopkins, Gary, "Has the Threat of Lawsuits Changed Our Schools?," *Education World*, September 28, 2004, https://www.educationworld.com/a_admin/admin/admin371.shtml

4. No author listed, "Qualified Immunity," Legal Information Institute, https://www.law.cornell.edu/wex/qualified_immunity

5. James, Bernard (Prof. of Law, Pepperdine University), "A Message from the Courts," June 24, 2021, https://www.nasro.org/news/2021/06/24/news-releases/qualified-immunity-in-public-education/

6. Barone, Richard, Steelhead, Amelia, "School District Neglect Results in $1,625,000 Verdict," law firm ad on web, https://www.rkmlaw.net/results/school-district-negligence-results-in-1625000-verdict/

Chapter 13

Labor Unions

Talking with most people about teacher labor unions evokes many negative comments. "They control everything in education; they have the legislature in their pockets." "They are a major reason our American public schools are in trouble." "They only care about their members and are not concerned about kids in school."

They resist change and have become an impediment to most proposals that move in the direction of improvement. This is the essence of what this chapter is all about. Yes, teacher unions are needed, but unions with a mission to help save the system rather than unions that persist in their current activities, activities that are helping to destroy it.

Disruptive children are killing our system. Teacher satisfaction is at an all-time low, well below the last data point recorded 11 years ago. Teachers are leaving at an accelerated rate because of a variety of reasons, money being only one of them. University students are not interested in becoming teachers. They see the videos of classroom conflict, they hear the stories of the lack of respect children have for their teachers, and they know that stepping into many classrooms is not a pleasant experience.

Where are the teacher unions? This is a plea for them to change direction and use their very powerful member organizations and huge political clout and funding to be a partner in major educational reform. Many Americans don't admire teacher unions, but they have a guarded respect for their power. Without change, they will be losing thousands of potential members and subjecting themselves to their own demise. America needs your help! You can be a strong positive force, not just for "quality" education but for the excellent system this country deserves.

DISCUSSION OF UNIONS

This book has painted a "not so pretty picture" of U.S. education. The system needs major reform; it is not working because it is not properly educating enough of our children. It is time to muster all influencers to meet the challenge to improve the system. Among the top influencers are teacher unions. Unfortunately, their influence has not been positive; in fact, it can be strongly negative, not necessarily for their members, but for the education system. Can unions be changed for the better?

Is this a fair assessment? Is there evidence to support it? Look at the mission of the two top teacher unions, the American Federation of Teachers (1.7 million members) and the National Education Association (3 million members).

AFT Mission:

The American Federation of Teachers is a union of professionals that champions fairness; democracy; economic opportunity; and high-quality public education, healthcare and public services for our students, their families, and our communities. We are committed to advancing these principles through community engagement, organizing, collective bargaining and political activism, and especially through the work our members do.[1]

NEA Mission and Core Values:

We, the members of the National Education Association of the United States, are the voice of education professionals. Our work is fundamental to the nation, and we accept the profound trust placed in us.[2]

CORE VALUES FOR NEA

These principles guide our work and define our mission. (These are listed because their mission statement is not specific about education.)

1. *Equal Opportunity.* We believe public education is the gateway to opportunity. All students have the human and civil right to a quality public education that develops their potential, independence, and character.
2. *A Just Society.* We believe public education is vital to building respect for the worth, dignity, and equality of every individual in our diverse society.

3. *Democracy.* We believe public education is the cornerstone of our republic. Public education provides individuals with the skills to be involved, informed, and engaged in our representative democracy.
4. *Professionalism.* We believe that the expertise and judgment of education professionals are critical to student success. We maintain the highest professional standards, and we expect the status, compensation, and respect due all professionals.
5. *Partnership.* We believe partnerships with parents, families, communities, and other stakeholders are essential to quality public education and student success.
6. *Collective Action.* We believe individuals are strengthened when they work together for the common good. As education professionals, we improve both our professional status and the quality of public education when we unite and advocate collectively.

Pull out the portions of these statements that are relevant to excellence in education. For the AFT it is "high-quality public education." For NEA it is "All students have the human and civil right to a quality public education" and "We maintain the highest professional standards, and we expect the status, compensation, and respect due all professionals." Both subscribe to the "quality public education" but what do they do to help promote a quality environment? Many of their comments focus on a good society, not a good school system. They sound more like a political party than a teacher union.

Unions must acknowledge that American students' performance is less than satisfactory. National assessment scores in math and reading have not changed in 48 years. Forty-seven percent of high school students are carrying an "A" average while their SAT scores are declining.

The inability to read properly will be a curse on many of these children for the remainder of their lives because, most likely, they will never catch up. Performance must improve; we are not producing children who will be competitive in the international race for wealth. The U.S. is losing badly to China, South Korea, Singapore, and so forth. The nation needs better trained students to fuel our nation's industrial plants. The U.S. is in trouble, and teacher unions are not helping to correct these vital issues.

So where are the teacher unions in all of this?

Do they fight for teacher working conditions in the classroom? Do they assist in the problems associated with disruptive children? Teachers would be a lot happier in their roles if they could get the time to teach the children rather that have it stolen away by discipline problems. Where are unions on these issues?

How can they stand to let this happen? How can they not support efforts to put their teachers in classrooms where they can teach rather than discipline children all day long? After all, if the U.S. public felt they were getting their money's worth for education, they might be willing to pay more.

IDEAS FROM THE EDUCATION LITERATURE

Are Labor Unions a Help or a Hindrance to Educational Excellence?

Here are several opinions on the value of teacher labor unions taken from the education literature. One thing to keep in mind is "value to who?" There are two targets to consider: (1) union members and (2) schoolchildren. It certainly is not true that what's good for union members will also benefit the education of our children.

These words come from an article from *Public School Review*.

The Benefits of Teacher Unions

When considering whether teacher unions provide real benefit to the student population, statistics may be a viable place to start. Two years ago, National Public Radio interviewed Randi Weingarten, president of AFT. Weingarten told NPR that schools in Singapore and Finland, which are 100% unionized, tend to perform better than U.S. schools. States that have more unionization, such as Massachusetts, New York, and Maryland, tend to perform better than those with less union participation, such as Mississippi and Louisiana, Weingarten told the Daily Beast.

Weingarten also told the Daily Beast that unions are the ticket to ensuring underserved students get the resources they need to perform academically. She explained, "Having a strong union, an entity that will look at what is done right and what is wrong and solve and change things, is the way to go."[3]

The fact of the matter is, with respect to the changes in Massachusetts, the unions tried many times to thwart the progressive changes in Massachusetts but could not get it done.

First, when it comes to state policy, the Massachusetts teachers' unions have been remarkably weak over the past fifteen years. They accepted the 1993 reform bill, as it came attached to hundreds of millions of dollars in new spending. But from all accounts it appears that they thought they'd be able to delete the reform elements over time. And they tried, battling the standards, the tests, the accountability, the higher standards for new teachers, the charter schools, everything.

And time and again, they lost. That's partly because Massachusetts had (an improbable) string of Republican governors in the 1990s and 2000s, and that's partly because of reform-minded Democratic legislators (like Tom Birmingham). And now that a Democrat has taken over the governor's chair, the union is starting to get its way.

Here's how Massachusetts reformer Jamie Gass explains it: What was unique about education reform in Massachusetts was that in addition to a great law, between 1993 and 2006, we had solid (bipartisan) state leaders like Tom Birmingham, Mark Roosevelt, Tom Finneran, Bill Weld, Paul Cellucci, John Silber, Abby Thernstrom, Roberta Schaefer, Mike Sentance, Sandy Stotsky, Bob Costrell, Jim Peyser, and Dave Driscoll. All these folks could and did say "no" to the unions for 15 years.

Having governors, legislative leaders, board of education members, and a commissioner who were aligned for the common purpose of improving student achievement and keeping the unions' strength in check made all the difference in Massachusetts.[4]

This quotation points out that the changes came about because unions were not allowed to have their way for an extended period. So, it happened despite the unions. With the presence of a democratic governor, the union is starting to get its way. The remarkable changes came about because the unions, though they tried, couldn't stop them!

THE PROBLEMS WITH TEACHER UNIONS

Not everyone agrees that teacher unions are the solution—in fact, in an age of serious education reform discussion, many believe they are the primary problem instead. In a report on Fox News, John Stossel states that unions may be good for teachers, but they are bad for students. He refers to an ex-police detective in New Jersey, Jim Smith, who now makes a living investigating "bad" teachers and working through the union-led process of firing them. He describes the process he went through to get rid of a teacher who allegedly hit students.

"It took me four years and $283,000–$127,000 in legal fees plus what it cost to have a substitute fill in, all the while he's sitting home having popcorn," Smith told Fox News.[5]

What are the pros of belonging to a teacher union?

1. *It protects teachers from political changes.*

    When the politics of a community or state change, education tends to be a popular department to address.

2. *It creates the possibility of tenure.*

Tenure is a misunderstood concept in the world of public education. It is often viewed as giving a teacher a "job for life," but that is
rarely the case.

3. *It creates unification.*

People working together can create change faster and better than
people working apart from one another.

4. *Schools with high levels of unionization tend to perform better.*

Countries that have 100% unionization levels in their schools, such
as Finland and Singapore, produce better results for their students than
schools in the United States

5. *Teachers can have a voice on policy.*

Teachers' unions allow individual teachers to be an advocate for
higher education spending. It gives them a voice in policy decisions
that would normally exclude their input but demand their compliance.

6. *Union fees are often tax deductible.*

What are the cons of teachers unions?

1. *Actions by unions can reduce educational opportunities for children.*
   Using children as a negotiation tool has its own set of ethical and
   moral considerations that must be individually addressed.
2. *It can lock districts into bad contracts over long periods.*
   For a collective bargaining agreement to be effective, both sides
   must send skilled negotiators to be part of the process of contract
   negotiation . . .
3. *The emphasis of the school changes.*
   Instead of emphasizing educational opportunities, teachers' unions
   are part of a process that changes the school into an economic opportunity. Children shouldn't be caught in the struggle between teachers and
   administrators who want resources in specific places.
4. *Unions may funnel funds to places that teachers do not support.*
5. *It creates a funding cycle that leaves taxpayers out of the equation.*

The government negotiates a salary with the teachers, who then have unions which advocate for the government officials.

6. *It can be costly to remove a bad teacher.*

Even when contracts allow for a bad teacher to be removed from the classroom, the process can be costly for the school district. In an interview with The Daily Beast, Terry Moe, a professor of political science at Stanford, said that it takes an average of $200,000 to remove just one poor teacher and up to 2 years of time to do so.[6]

Here's more from Terry Moe, PhD, a professor at Stanford University and a longtime foe of teacher unions:

Why are America's public schools failing? Why, after more than a quarter century of perpetual reform, has the nation been unable to bring real change to public education? While a complete answer, of course, would be very complicated. But at the heart of it lies the power of the teachers' unions—the National Education Association, the American Federation of Teachers, and their state and local affiliates.

I don't say this out of some sort of anti-union ideology. I say it as an objective description of the reality, backed by an enormous amount of data. *Union power has created insurmountable problems for effective schools.*

The purpose of a union is to represent the job interests of its members, and these interests are simply not the same as the interests of children. How, then, do they pursue these job interests? They do it in two ways.

The first is through collective bargaining, which takes place in local school districts. Through collective bargaining, the unions can win countless restrictive work rules, written into binding contracts that specify how the schools must be organized. Typically, for example, these contracts include salary rules requiring that teachers be paid entirely based on seniority and credentials, without any regard for whether their students are learning anything.

Often, these contracts also include seniority rules that allow senior teachers to take desirable jobs when they come open—even if these teachers are mediocre in the classroom or a bad fit for the school. There are also seniority rules requiring that, in layoff situations, excellent young teachers must be let go—automatically—and their senior colleagues must be kept on no matter how incompetent they may be. Labor contracts are just filled with these kinds of perverse rules. No one who's thinking only of what is best for kids would ever organize the schools in this way.

The other way teachers' unions shape the public schools is through the political process—where they simply have far more clout than any other education groups, by many orders of magnitude. They have over four million members, they're top contributors to political campaigns, they have armies of activists in the electoral trenches, they have lobbying organizations in all fifty states, and much more.

They have used this political clout to block or substantially weaken major reforms.

For decades, for example, reformers have tried to bring accountability to America education, but the unions have stood in the way.

As Arne Duncan well expressed, the nation is fully aware that it has a problem with its public schools. But the main reason that problem persists is that there's another problem, a more fundamental one that prevents real change and improvement—the problem of union power. Until the nation can recognize that problem—and do something about it—America's public schools will never be organized to provide kids with the most effective education possible.[7]

WRAPPING UP

The labor unions are watching the U.S. education system collapse around them, leaving American schools and students as mediocre players in the world's largest competition, the competition for wealth.

Students around the world are working much harder and learning more in a shorter period than American public-school kids. Nations such as China, South Korea, and Singapore are prospering, they have better schools and deliver more qualified employees to their industries. Of course, America is prospering, but in time, America will lose more and more small battles and capital will flow to other countries.

The education world is crumbling as teachers' unions watch. They should use their tremendous organizational skills and power to join in the effort to develop an excellent system. They should use their skills to set and enforce academic standards. They should endorse excellent teachers and excellent teaching.

NOTES

1. American Federation of Teachers website: https://www.aft.org/about/mission

2. National Education Association website: https://www.nea.org/about-nea/mission-vision-values

3. Chen, Grace, "Are Teacher Unions a Help or Hindrance to Public Education?," *Public School Review*, May 18, 2022, https://www.publicschoolreview.com/blog/are-teacher-unions-a-help-or-hindrance-to-public-education

4. Petrilli, Michael J., "What Does the Massachusetts Miracle Teach Us About Teacher Unions?," Thomas Fordham Institute, May 18, 2009, https://fordhaminstitute

.org/national/commentary/what-does-massachusetts-miracle-teach-us-about-teachers
-unions

5. Op. cit., Chen, Grace.

6. Gaille, Louis, "13 Pros and Cons of Teacher Unions," *Vittian Personal Finance*,
August 1, 2017, https://vittana.org/13-pros-and-cons-of-teachers-unions

7. Moe, Terry, "Teacher Unions vs Students," Prager U, https://assets.ctfassets.net
/qnesrjodfi80/2Ux8fqBbTGW6sk42c4yuuk/69220ec2dacdd2039f17e020880ac5b5/
moe-teachers_unions_vs_students-transcript.pdf

Chapter 14

The Massachusetts Education Miracle and the Maryland Commission

Lessons can be learned from places where success has been achieved. Within the United States a notable success story can be derived from what and how the state of Massachusetts changed their education system in the early 1990s.

Another interesting case is the state of Maryland and its reform program that is in the early stages of implementation. Measuring its success is many years away, so it is impossible to say what is going to happen. Turn to a common concept derived from industry: "Good processes produce good outcomes." Maryland is setting up a good process and will most likely have good outcomes.

SUPERIOR EDUCATIONS PRODUCE PAYBACK

Dr. Andreas Schleicher, PhD, is a German mathematician, statistician, and researcher in the field of education. As the leader of PISA, he knows more about international education than anyone on earth. He says: "The quality of schooling in a country is a reliable predictor of the wealth that country will produce in the long run."

Dr. Schleicher is talking about countries in his quotation, but his statement can also be applied to states. Consider what happened in Massachusetts over the 25-year period from 1993 to 2018. In 1993, Massachusetts passed their 1993 Education Reform Act, and soon after held the number one rank among all states. Just as Dr. Schleicher points out in his quotation, benefits accrue to states as well. See table 14.1.

Starting at about the same per capita income in 1993, the per capita difference in 2018 between the two states is $8,329. The population of

Table 14.1. Personal Income Per Capita

Personal Income Per Capita			
	1993	2018	Percentage Change
Maryland	$25,239	$63,354	151%
Massachusetts	$25,471	$71,683	181%

Massachusetts in 2018 was 6.88 million. Thus, the tax base of Massachusetts was $57.44 billion more than Maryland for that year alone. There were gains in most of the 25-year period. A spreadsheet analysis shows a total 25-year gain of $457 billion in taxable revenue.

This increase delivered billions to the Massachusetts tax revenues. Maryland is counting on this same effect from their new reform program. These gains are available to other states if they can improve their education system.

THE MASSACHUSETTS EDUCATION MIRACLE

For about thirteen years, Massachusetts has been ranked the best state for K-12 education using test scores from the U.S. Department of Education's National Assessment Educational Progress (NAEP).[1] On international tests administered by PISA (Program for International Student Assessment) which only ranks countries, if Massachusetts were a country, it would rank in the top 10. By any measure they are outstanding educators.

MASSACHUSETTS HISTORY ON EDUCATIONAL REFORM

The Massachusetts state constitution requires the state as follows: "it shall be the duty of legislatures and magistrates, in all future periods of this commonwealth, to cherish . . . the public schools and grammar schools in the towns." In 1978, a complaint was filed against the state, arguing there were significant differences in funding across the state's school districts, differences that were not allowed under the state constitution.

The complaint asked that these differences be eliminated. The handwriting was on the wall for Massachusetts to change the system before the court ruling changed it for you. A group of businessmen decided to take charge of the situation and restructure the system before the Supreme Court issued its ruling:

> In 1991, businessman Jack Rennie and the Massachusetts Business Alliance for Education (MBAE) produced an influential report that proposed a foundation budget, as well as increased state authority in setting standards, incentives, and penalties. The report was the basis of the 1993 Foundation Budget, passed by the legislature and signed by the governor.
>
> It recommended that "a broad array of performance indicators should be developed, not simply results of standardized tests." It anticipated broad turnaround powers for superintendents in underperforming schools, including replacing staff and potentially privatizing functions such as foreign language instruction. It recommended a graduation test requirement as well as improvements that have not been widely adopted but are still recommended; pre-school for all 3- and 4-year-olds; parent outreach and education; extended learning time; school-based authorities; teacher recruitment, especially of minority candidates; integration of social services; increased vocational education; and professional development.[2]

In 1993, the Massachusetts Supreme Court ruled on the case. Here is a summary of a judgment made against the state:

> In June 1993, the Massachusetts Supreme Judicial Court issued its decision in *McDuffy v. Secretary of the Executive Office of Education*, 415 Mass. 545, 615 N.E.2d 516 (1993). The decision established the state constitutional standards against which education reform efforts in Massachusetts would be judged.
>
> The complaint, which was initiated in 1978 and amended in 1990, was brought on behalf of students in certain property-poor communities who alleged that the school finance system violated the education clause of the Massachusetts Constitution. In words unchanged since 1780, the education clause states in part that "[i]t shall be the duty of legislatures and magistrates, in all future periods of this commonwealth, to cherish . . . the public schools and grammar schools in the towns." Mass. Const., pt. II, ch. V, § II.
>
> The plaintiffs claimed that the Commonwealth had failed its constitutional duty to provide them with the opportunity to receive an adequate education of sufficiently high quality.[3]

To clarify, the outcome of this ruling sets the requirement that the state equitably fund all school districts. This means that property-rich school districts will no longer dominate in school funding. Low property value districts will be funded by both property taxes and other state monies.

THE MASSACHUSETTS EDUCATION
REFORM ACT OF 1993

As a result of the Business Alliance, and Jack Rennie's leadership and report, the legislature came forward with the reform act of 1993 thereby providing a remedy for the Supreme Court's ruling.

> The Massachusetts Education Reform Act (MERA) of 1993 was intended to provide a more equal education for children throughout the state. The MERA has been described as a "grand bargain," increasing state financial assistance to local schools dramatically in return for greater state control through state standards and measures, and for greater parent choice through charter schools and inter-district choice.[4]

Here is a summary description of the Massachusetts Education Reform Act of 1993:

> The Act calls for dramatic changes in public education over a seven-year period. Among the major provisions of the Act are greater and more equitable funding to schools, accountability for student learning, and statewide standards for students, educators, schools, and districts. By the end of this decade, the Secretary of Education estimates that more than $2 billion in new state Education Reform will have been provided to Massachusetts public schools because of the Act's provisions.
>   Some of the major changes in accountability proposed in the Education Reform Act included these requirements: a school council in every school,[5] continuing education for educators, more authority for every principal, better defined roles for school committees, and clear, concise, and measurable statewide standards for students and schools. The capstone is a "high-stakes" test based on the new curriculum standards which every student needs to pass to receive a diploma.[6]

The following outlines some of the major provisions of the 1993 Massachusetts Education Reform Act as passed.

Creation of the "Common Core"

The common core lays out what each student needs to learn in each grade.

Statewide Student Testing

The new statewide test, the Massachusetts Comprehensive Assessment System (MCAS), was created with the intention of reflecting the academic standards in the curriculum frameworks. The purpose of the test is to identify individuals and schools which need attention in particular areas. The Act requires that the tests be given to students in grades 4, 8 and 10.

Graduation Standards

The Act mandates that all students pass the state's tenth-grade test, in addition to meeting local requirements, to receive a diploma. The Act also includes provisions that would allow students passing the new tenth-grade test to receive additional certificates in the future—the Certificate of Occupational Proficiency or a Certificate of Mastery. The academic standards for receiving these certificates are not outlined in the legislation but were promulgated by the Board and Commissioner of Education.

Time and Learning

Under the Education Reform Act, emphasis was placed on increasing the amount of learning time in schools. Districts are required to submit their plans to schedule students for at least 900 hours in elementary schools and 990 hours in secondary schools to study the core academic subjects.

Teacher Testing

The Education Reform Act emphasizes raising expectations for all educators, both new to teaching as well as veterans. The Act requires that, beginning in 1998, all new teachers are required to pass two tests to become certified to teach in Massachusetts public schools

District Performance

The Act allows the Board and Commissioner to formulate criteria to determine school and district performance. Under the Education Reform Act, if a district is found to be "under-performing," the state can take it into receivership.[7]

This is an excellent list of system requirements, all of which are important. In the author's opinion some are more important than others. Here are the key requirements, the things that make this reform act work:

1. Clear, concise, and measurable statewide standards for students and schools.
2. The Act mandates that all students pass the state's tenth-grade test, in addition to meeting local requirements, to receive a diploma.
3. The academic standards for receiving these certificates are not outlined in the legislation but were promulgated by the Board and Commissioner of Education.

THE MARYLAND COMMISSION

The state of Maryland has undertaken a massive reform of their K-12 public schools. Since the full implementation of their plan is probably 12 to 15 years away, it will take at least that long to graduate their first classes. Looking at this study will reveal excellent data about how they went about drawing their conclusions and justifying their proposals. One study is of particular interest and that is the financial analysis of the costs and benefits of the proposed revised program.

The state of Maryland had a proud history as a top state for many years. They stood by and watched as Massachusetts reformed their system and shot to the top of the Top School Systems in the U.S. They were headed in the other direction and decided to act.

In 2016 the Maryland Commission on Innovation & Excellence in Education was formed, and Dr. William Kirwan was asked to take the lead role. Dr. Kirwan was a highly regarded educational leader in Maryland holding his final position as chancellor of the Maryland University System, a position he held from 2002 until 2015. His career has other notable accomplishments. Dr. Kirwan worked at the University of Maryland, College Park, from the 1960s to 1990s as a professor, administrator, and eventually president, and was president of the Ohio State University from 1998 to 2002.

Henceforth, the Maryland Commission on Innovation and Excellence in Education will be named the Kirwan Commission. Here is a bit more history of the commission that is drawn from their 2020 final report:

> The Commission on Innovation and Excellence in Education was created in 2016 as a bi-partisan effort by Governor Lawrence J. Hogan, Jr. and the General Assembly. The Commission was asked to assess the current state of Maryland's PreK-12 education system and the adequacy of its funding formulas *and* to make policy and resource recommendations that would ensure Maryland children achieve at the levels of students in the world's best-performing school systems.
>
> The premise for the creation of the Commission and its charge was driven in large part by the widely accepted view that success in today's economy requires a well-educated, highly skilled workforce. The ability of Maryland enterprises, from family farms to medical technology companies, to be competitive requires their access to a workforce with world-class technical expertise and a general education that enables individuals to master ever changing, complex new skills quickly and easily.
>
> Moreover, the State's responsibility to make broadly shared prosperity for its citizens possible depends as never before on the ability of its education system and its students to meet world class education standards.
>
> Most of the commissioners began their work assuming that Maryland already had an outstanding education system, but we quickly discovered that data do not

support that conclusion. We learned that while Maryland has some fine schools and excellent teachers, it does not have nearly enough of either. Indeed, failing schools exist in every jurisdiction across the State.

The Commission's most troubling findings include the following:

- Maryland students perform at or below the median among the 50 states in the National Assessment of Educational Progress (NAEP) exams, given to fourth and eighth graders in reading and mathematics, among other grades and subjects. Since the same exams are given in every state, they are called the Nation's Report Card and offer the best comparative assessment of student performance among the 50 states. In 2019, the most recent NAEP scores, Maryland ranked 32nd in fourth grade math, 25th in fourth grade reading, 28th in eighth grade math, and 17th in eighth grade reading. Even more troubling, Maryland's scores have fallen significantly over the past decade.
- Maryland is considered a regressive state in terms of school funding . . . one respected source of funding equity analysis is the Education Law Center (ELC) at Rutgers University. . . . By this measure, ELC ranks Maryland as the 11th most regressive state in the United States.
- Maryland has unacceptably large achievement gaps based on race and income. According to the most recent assessment results from Maryland State Department of Education (MSDE), roughly 50% of white students are deemed proficient in Algebra I upon high school graduation (a distressingly low number), whereas only 12.5% of Hispanic and 11.4% of African American students achieve at this level. The gaps are similar in English language arts. Roughly 56% of white students but only 24% of African American and Hispanic students achieve the proficiency level by the time they graduate.[8]

These poor performance results were a shock to a state that was, all along, comparing themselves to other mediocre states. It was discovered when they "dug down" into the available data that they found they were not even close to where they thought they were and even farther away from where they would like to be.

Their College and Career Ready number was around 40% meaning that only 40% of their graduating seniors were properly prepared to attend college or a trade school. It's no wonder the state's businesses were having trouble filling their positions, positions that demand better training than in the past. The commission set a CCR goal of 80% that would be attained upon full implementation of their new system.

One of the sources of knowledge that proved valuable to the commission study teams was the engagement of the National Center on Education and Economy (NCEE). NCEE is a highly regarded not-for-profit organization that has spent the past 30 years doing comparative analyses of school systems around the world. The NCEE was founded by Marc Tucker, one of the leading U.S. experts who can blend the best of the international's top systems to meet the needs of U.S. systems. They were instrumental in the formulation of the Commission's report.

Here are some of the highlights of their proposed system. These are the five policy areas that make up the totality of their recommendations.[9]

Policy Area 1. Early Childhood Education

- Free prekindergarten for all low income, 3- and 4-year-old children; available to other children on a sliding scale. The objective is to prepare all children for learning as kindergarten students
- Public funding for these schools
- To provide the needed prekindergarten teachers, a substantial increase in the supply of early childhood education teachers through tuition assistance and financial support for those pursuing credentials and degrees; and
- To supply needed services for the very young students, an expansion of both Family Support Centers for pre- and post-natal support and Judy Centers for early childhood education and family support, and full funding of the Infants and Toddlers Program to identify early candidates and provide supports to young children with disabilities

Policy Level 2. High Quality and Diverse Teachers and School Leaders

- To elevate teachers to respectable levels, to draw people from the general labor pool into the classroom, and to raise average teacher pay from the then average Maryland pay of $64,600 to $80,461. This level makes the teacher's position competitive with other jobs that require a four-year university degree.
- Make teacher education more rigorous
- Provide a career ladder for teachers that places approximately 12% of a school's teacher staff into these three levels: Lead Teacher, Master Teacher, and Professor Master Teacher
- Provide a leadership development system that prepares school leaders at all levels—state, district, and school—to give them the vision, skills, and knowledge they need to implement the recommendations made in the Commission's report and manage high-performing schools.

Policy Level 3. College and Career Readiness Pathways

- Develop a system that will allow most students to complete the common core in 10 years instead of 12. For students planning to attend a university, the remaining two years will be focused on college courses. For students working for skill certifications, the last two years focus on a rigorous technical education leading to industry-recognized credentials and high-paying jobs.
- Setting the College and Career Readiness Standard (CCR) to global standards that certifies that those who reach it have the required literacy in English and mathematics (and when practicable, science) to succeed in first-year credit-bearing courses.
- Development of a Career Technical Education (CTE) system that will propel graduates into positions that will support the state's economic future.

Policy Level 4. More Resources to Ensure That All Students Are Successful

- Additional funding for English Learners (EL) students, including EL family coordinators.
- Creating a new program for schools with high concentrations of students living in poverty, in addition to student-based funding through the compensatory education formula. The new Concentration of Poverty School Grants would fund community schools that coordinate needed social services, before- and after-school and summer academic programs and expanded student access to school-based health services. In addition to a base amount for each school, the amount of additional funding would be based on the concentration of poverty in a school above 55%.
- Establishing a Transitional Supplemental Instruction for Struggling Learners program to provide additional funding for one-on-one and small-group instruction for students who Blueprint for Maryland's Future: Building a World-class Education System in Maryland
- Are not, or are not on track to, reading at grade level by grade 3 (secondarily students who are not proficient in math). These funds are provided over a six-year period, ultimately phasing out as other components of the new education system are implemented, including more time outside the classroom for teachers to provide personalized instruction to students who need additional supports.

Policy Level 5. Governance and Accountability

The list of activities related to Policy Level 5 will not be shown in all its detail. The list is a commonsense set of activities required to implement and monitor activities for compliance for the new system while in operation. One of the keys to success is accountability; they have assigned accountability and will hold people/schools accountable.

RETURN OF INVESTMENT ANALYSIS

As a nation we have grown accustomed to free public education and don't give much thought to analyzing the payback that accrues to the country. The Maryland study presents a unique opportunity to look at this issue. In simple terms, look at it this way; if a dollar is spent on education, what is the return on this dollar? Is it more than $1 or less?

Maryland has many graduating high school seniors who are not prepared to attend either a university or a "trade school." Recall that only 40% of Maryland high school graduates are CCR; leaving 60% who are not ready for college or a career path. What happens to these students in the future? Some will realize the folly of their ways and find a way to fill in for their missing educations and get a job. Many will take minimum wage jobs; some will do nothing and just barely survive.

Others will end up on food stamps, Medicaid, and other public support programs. Still others will get in trouble with the law and end up in jail. These latter folks are spending government dollars, not paying taxes, and are a "drain" on the treasury.

Refresh our memories: How big a problem is crime for high school dropouts?

HIGH SCHOOL DROPOUTS ARE MORE LIKELY TO TURN TO CRIME

High school dropouts are three and one-half times more likely than high school graduates to be arrested, and more than eight times as likely to be incarcerated. Across the country, 68 percent of state prison inmates have not received a high school diploma.

According to researchers, 10 percentage-point increases in graduation rates have historically been shown to reduce murder and assault rates by approximately 20 percent. Increasing graduation rates by 10 percentage points would prevent over 3,000 murders and nearly 175,000 aggravated assaults in America each year.[10]

Suppose the new Maryland reform measures do meet their goal CCR of 80%. This will place many more viable candidates into universities and vocational schools. These folks will get good jobs and pay taxes; they will not need food stamps, rental assistance, Medicaid, and they will not go to jail. This is a win-win deal; they pay money into government and do not need government support.

A LOOK AT THE ECONOMICS OF
THE MARYLAND PROPOSAL

In 2019, Strong Schools Maryland[11] released a report titled "An Economic Assessment of Kirwan Commission Recommendations."[12] This was the Return on Investment (ROI) report supporting the Maryland reform program. This report determined that annual costs equaled annual benefits 14 years after the initiation of the program in 2020. The breakeven point, when the benefits covered all costs up to that point, at 25 years. Once at steady state, the return to Maryland was $1.66 for every dollar spent.

In April 2022, Strong Schools Maryland released an update to the 2019 study titled "An Updated Economic and Fiscal Assessment of Education Reform in Maryland."[13] The new report considers inflation, a slower implementation and changed some assumptions. This analysis begins implementation in 2021 and annual costs equals annual benefit after 11 years; the breakeven point is reached after 18 years. The cost benefit ratio varies over time; at year 11 it is $1.08 for every dollar spent, at 18 years, breakeven, it is $2.11 for ever dollar spent.

After 25 years it is $2.49 for every dollar spent. After 25 years it slows down and begins to flatten out. After 18 years, the newly minted seniors have yet to enter the labor market and earn a decent wage. Needing to pick one cost benefit ratio for this book, pick $2.20 for every dollar spent. This is an excellent return for Maryland and one of the reasons they are moving forward. The dollar amounts are quite large; the average annual expenditure for years 10 to 20 is $5.1 billion, and the average annual benefit is $11.3 billion.

As Maryland calculated their reform benefits, they were realistic about student uptake. Today their College and Career Readiness number is 40%. Their long-term CCR goal number is 80%. They never assumed that *all* graduates were either going to college or would be pursuing a certificate of career readiness in some field. They selected the more realistic 80% and it would get there over time. They also made careful assumptions as to what percent would attend a university and what percent would go to a vocational school. Their analysis doesn't seem to "pack the deck" in favor of reform.

What is not discussed (regarding Massachusetts and Maryland) are the large intangible benefits of a great education system. Once students are surrounded by other students who are performing at high levels it will motivate them to attain higher goals. They will learn that education is its own reward, meaning that knowledge brings self-confidence, elevated self-esteem, and the acknowledgment that "I can get a piece of the action." Chapter 16 lists a few intangible benefits that accrue to a country that has an excellent education system.

Both case studies have given insight into "the art of the possible." Massachusetts shows that we Americans have the intellectual capability to perform at a high level if placed into a well-designed education system. This was never in doubt, but as a nation, the U.S. is not living up to our potential. The Maryland study shows the way for another state to repeat the process and do their own study. It also presents a good return on investment, an analysis that is relatively rare in education.

NOTES

1. Norton, Michael, "Mass. Students Still Rank at or Near the Top, but NAEP Scores Show Decline," *The New Bedford Light*, October 25, 2022, https://newbedfordlight .org/mass-students-still-rank-at-or-near-top-but-naep-scores-show-decline/

2. Jahlen, Patricia zd. (state senator), "Rethinking School Accountability: Opportunities for Massachusetts Under Every Student Succeeds Act," State of Massachusetts, May 2018, https://btu.org/wp-content/uploads/2018/05/Senator_Jehlen_ESSA _Subcommittee_Report_May2018.pdf

3. Schneider, Rhoda (Gen. Counsel, Mass. Dept of Education), "The State Constitutional Mandate for Education: The McDuffy and Handcock Decisions," Mass. Dept of Elementary and Secondary Education, no date given, https://www.doe.mass.edu/ lawsregs/litigation/mcduffy-hancock.html

4. Jahlen, Patrica D. (state senator), "Rethinking School Accountability," May 2018.

5. A school council is a representative, school building-based committee composed of the principal, parents, teachers, community members and, at the secondary level, students, required to be established by each school pursuant to Massachusetts General Laws Chapter 71, Section 59C, often called a School Board.

6. Gass, Jamie, Chieppo, Charles, "How Massachusetts Showed the Way on Education Reform," The Pioneer Institute, May 16, 2019, https://pioneerinstitute.org/ common_core/how-massachusetts-showed-the-way-on-education-reform/

7. Overview of the Massachusetts Education Reform Act of 1993, Adapted from the Secretary of Education's Progress Report, May 1997 by the Francis W. Parker Charter Essential School's Regional Teachers Center.

8. "Blueprint for Maryland's Future, Final Report 2020," Maryland Commission on Innovation and Excellence in Education, Final Report, December 2020, https://dls

.maryland.gov/pubs/prod/NoPblTabMtg/CmsnInnovEduc/2020-Final-Report-of-the
-Commission.pdf

9. Ibid.

10. Christenson, Bill, Lee, Brian, et al., "School on the Streets, Crime
and America's Dropout Crisis," Fight Crime, Invest in Kids," 2008, https://
alabamapartnershipforchildren.org/wp-content/uploads/2016/12/School-or-the
-Streets-Crime-and-Americas-Dropout-Crisis.pdf

11. Strong Schools Maryland, https://www.strongschoolsmaryland.org/about-us

12. This report is no longer available.

13. Strong Schools Maryland, look under Resources/ROI Report 2022, use website
above. Use exhibit 9 on page 19.

Chapter 15

Overhead, a Constant Threat

Education requires funding, and hopefully, decisions are made that will fund teacher's salaries and other delivery expenses, rather than overhead. Care must be exerted to be sure overhead does not grow too rapidly.

What is overhead? In a business it is:

$$\text{Total Expenses} - \text{Direct Expenses} = \text{Overhead}$$

WHAT ARE OVERHEAD COSTS?

Overhead costs refer to those expenses associated with running a business that can't be directly linked to creating or producing a product or service. They are the expenses the business incurs to stay in business, regardless of its success level.

Overhead costs are all the costs on the company's income statement except for those that are directly related to manufacturing or selling a product or providing a service. For example, a potter's clay and potting wheel are not overhead costs because they are directly related to the products made. The rent for the facility where the potter creates is an overhead cost because the potter pays rent whether they are creating products or not.

OVERHEAD COST EXAMPLES

A company's overhead costs depend on the nature of the business. A retailer's expenses will be different from a repair shop or a craftsman. Typical examples include:

- Rent
- Utilities
- Insurance

- Salaries that aren't job- or product-specific
- Office equipment such as computers or telephones
- Office supplies[1]

In a business all monies must go somewhere. One of the important places for it to go is to the cost of the products sold. Here are two of these costs: direct materials and direct labor. Consider a plant that makes only two products. In this case it is allowable to spread the cost of the factory management, plant electrical bill, and so forth., directly to the two products in proportion to the volume of each. One product might require 90% of the manager's total pay, plus secretary, to be added to the product cost.

WHAT ABOUT SCHOOLS?

What are the direct costs of teaching an elementary school student? It would certainly be teacher salaries plus salaries of teaching assistants who work with teachers in their room. Would it include part of the electric bill? Most likely not. Schools have exterior lights; the bill for these is allocatable to the classroom, but it is not a direct cost.

Keeping overhead down is a constant battle; there are always "nice things to do," but are they essential? This is a persistent upper management problem. Larry Arnn, president of Hillsdale College, published a report including figure 15.1:[2]

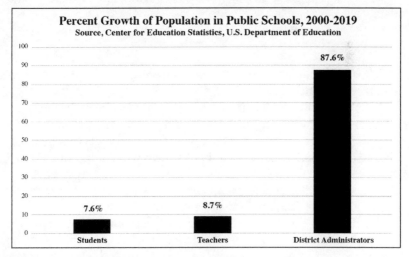

Figure 15.1. Percentage Growth of Population in Public Schools 2000–2019
Source: Center for Educational Statistics U.S. Department of Education

What in the world is happening to the District Administrator costs? Since almost all these folks are in the overhead category, isn't this a case of runaway spending?

Here is more detail for the tall bar.[3] The District Administrator's bar is made up of two components: Officials & Administrator growth over period is 135%, and Instruction Coordinators growth over period is 265%. Both bars look suspicious: the first grew over 10 times faster than students or teachers; the second grew 33 times faster. This category began in 2000 with 39,433 people and ended 2018 with 95,746, a growth of 56,300 people.

Assume their salary cost with benefits is $120,000/year, then this is an additional cost of $6.8 million. This looks like runaway overhead. The only folks who can stop it are the local school boards. They should fight to give these funds to teachers, not administrate staff.

A CASE STUDY FROM ILLINOIS

Illinoisans face the second-highest property tax rates in the nation, with the bulk of those taxes going to schools. They spend among the most per student in the Midwest on education, but student outcomes lag many of the state's neighbors.

Why? Too many education dollars get trapped in bureaucracy before reaching the classroom. *In the past four years, Illinois public schools employed fewer teachers and had fewer students, but the number of administrators grew.*

Illinois spent $8.4 billion on public education in its fiscal year 2019 budget, not including pension costs for the Teachers' Retirement System. Too much of that money is propping up a system with 852 school districts—one of the nation's highest counts. Staffing those districts are over 9,000 school administrators who in 2017 earned over $100,000 per year, and they'll each receive $3 million or more in pension benefits during their retirements.[4]

In the above case, multiply the 9,000 school administrators by $100,000 gives $900 million in overhead costs.

The problem is Illinois puts its money into too many administrators running too many school districts. By consolidating school districts without closing schools, Illinois can improve college readiness and save taxpayers money. If Illinois pursued reforms suggested by the Metropolitan Planning Council, and reduced general administration spending to the national average, Illinois could save $708 million annually—double the new money put toward education when the school funding formula was rewritten in 2017.

Solving this problem is up to the legislature. It is hard to imagine a school district saying, "Lets consolidate with the other schools in the county and have only one superintendent's office. Perhaps, if someone took hold of this issue to show them the tax savings, they might agree to do it.

CASE STUDY FROM WISCONSIN

The last two state budgets significantly increased K-12 funding, but the proportion spent in classrooms has slightly dipped.

Data from the Department of Public Instruction (DPI) show that just 53.6% of K-12 spending goes toward classroom instruction. Despite record-high increases to education funding, the percentage of dollars reaching the classroom has fallen slightly compared to the prior year.

Schools have taken on numerous roles outside of the instruction of students, and the budget allocations reflect that reality. If top-heavy overhead were reduced, perhaps the teachers doing most meaningful work in schools could be better compensated.

The second-highest category of spending is on "operations/other," a catch-all category that captures 13.4% of spending, or $1,811 per student. That category includes items such as central services, maintenance, debt service, insurance, and post-employment benefit debt.[5]

The key point to this last case is that funding is going to overhead and being taken away from instruction. This is difficult to understand; teachers need to be paid more. One wonders when looking at data like this, how much of the debt funding and overhead is going to spectacular athletic facilities instead of the business at hand, changing children's lives.

NOTES

1. No author listed, "Overhead Costs," Shopify, https://www.shopify.com/encyclopedia/overhead-costs

2. Arnn, Larry P., "Education as a Battleground," *Imprimis*, November 2022, https://imprimis.hillsdale.edu/education-as-a-battleground/

3. "Table 213.10 Staff employed in public elementary and secondary school systems," the latest version, NCES (National Center for Educational Statistics), https://nces.ed.gov/programs/digest/d19/tables/dt19_213.10.asp

4. Divounguy, Orphe, Schuster, Adam, Hill, Bryce, "Bureaucrats Over Classroom: Illinois Wastes Millions of Education Dollars on Unnecessary Layers of Administration," *Illinois Policy*, no date given, https://www.illinoispolicy.org/reports/bureaucrats-over-classrooms-illinois-wastes-millions-of-education-dollars-on-unnecessary-layers-of-administration/

5. Lisowski, Lisa, "As K12 Education Funding Jumps Dramatically, Still Just 54% of Funding Spent on Instruction," MacIver Institute, March 5, 2020, https://www.maciverinstitute.com/2020/03/as-school-spending-rises-just-54-of-funding-spent-on-instruction/

Chapter 16

National Impact

What is the national impact of a dramatically improved education system? The impact can be divided into tangible (economic) impacts and intangible gains. As is shown below, the economic gains can be huge for a single state and one can arrive at gigantic gains when multiple states are simultaneously working on changes.

ECONOMIC GAINS

Before looking at economic gains, consider economic losses. The U.S. already spends 35% more on PreK-12 education than the average of the developed nations. Since the country is not performing well, this extra 35% is not paying off. The country now spends $764.7 billion on public K-12 education from all sources.[1] This is $15,120 per student. What part of this is overhead? That number is not readily available, but there is a touch point in a paper about overhead in Wisconsin.[2] In Wisconsin, 54% of their education budget goes to teaching, so the other 46% is overhead. Since there is no solid data on this, speculation is not allowed.

This portion is an abbreviated recap of some of the results given in chapter 14. Chapter 14 examined the Maryland State reform program. The ROI (Return on Investment) of this program is a return of $2.20 for every new $1 spent on education for each year. Recall this analysis computed the reduction in state costs from fewer people going on food stamps, Medicaid, rental assistance, and energy subsidies; fewer people incarcerated; and the sizable increases in state and federal tax revenue since these former students are now working.

The gains are over and above what was already happening in the state. Looking at Maryland again shows in their new program they are spending $5.1 billion[3] *more* each year (at steady state) and for that money, they reap a benefit of $11.3 billion in an average year (project years 15 to 25). Divide

$11.3 by $5.1 to get the $2.20 for every dollar spent. This number can be used to compute most any state or national impact one wants to present. This financial data was presented in chapter 14.

ANOTHER APPROACH

In 2018 alone, there is a per capita income difference of $8,349 favoring Massachusetts.[4] Multiplying this by the Massachusetts population of 6.88 million gives an increase in taxable income of $57.44 billion. Using this approach for each of the 26 years, and adding up all the annual gains, gives the state of Massachusetts a $457 billion taxable income advantage over Maryland. The Massachusetts reform was driven by higher standards, so it wasn't as expensive as Maryland's program, allowing them to "bank" more of the taxes from this gain.

Make reform assumptions and compute the national economic gain and it is possible to produce gigantic numbers, but this path will not be followed; it's too speculative.

INTANGIBLE GAINS

America used to stand tall for its education prowess. Foreign delegations visited to see how the country delivered free, quality public education. The country has entered an educational slide that seems to be gaining speed. This slide must stop, and the ship must be turned around. Drastic actions must be taken to stop runaway discipline problems, standards must be established to drive our education up to new heights of performance.

Intangible Benefits of an Excellent K-12 System

1. Preserve Democracy: The U.S. education system is slipping and consequently so is our democracy. When looking at the January 6th riot at the U.S. capitol, it seems many of the rioters were misled by their own leaders and the president. A well-educated population will think more for themselves rather than let errant leaders think for them. Education is the bulwark of democracy; poor education leads to a weak democracy.
2. National and Personal Pride: A well-informed citizenry has self-confidence and a sense of pride both in themselves and the nation. Education creates self-confidence and self-esteem. It promotes equality and equalizes class differences.

3. Establish a Solid Basis for Never Ending Learning: Good reading skills are essential for continued learning. These skills will best be learned in a formal school system. Basic reading skills must be in place before entering the fourth grade. From that point until the end of life, these skills should serve our people and our country well.

4. Restore Faith in Government: Faith in governmental institutions is declining. Schools are certainly part of this "lack of confidence." A revitalized public school system would have monumental benefits for everyone. It wouldn't be nearly as necessary to pick a neighborhood with a good system; most systems will be satisfactory.

5. Supply Employment Needs: A solid education system provides candidates to take jobs within the U.S. economy. Today a huge number of high school graduates do not have the skills to do most well paid jobs nor are they candidates for military careers. Employment will boost the U.S. standard of living and bring many otherwise wards of the state into self-sufficiency. The military will find more qualified candidates.

6. Elevate the Status of Teachers: The status and respect for teachers is at an all-time low. Paying teachers more in line with other four-year university graduates and having well-managed classrooms will elevate the status of the profession.

7. International Competition: America's position in the international economy has always been at the top. Every day, students around the world go to school and develop skills that will help push their economies forward in the wealth race. America must be competitive in this race or wealth will move away from U.S. shores.

8. A Better Society: more self-sufficiency; fewer food stamps, rent subsidies, Medicaid, and so on. "The link between a poor education and incarceration is borne out in data. Dropouts are 3.5 times more likely to be arrested than high school graduates. Nationally, 68 percent of all males in prison do not have a high school diploma."[5]

Wrapping Up

There is no doubt that the current slide in American education is eating at the nation's soul. Folks talk about it all the time, telling "You can't believe what happened in class today" stories. Stories about teachers retiring early, about teachers advising young people to never become a teacher. Without strong leadership and a massive mobilization, nothing is going to change. It is long past time to start.

NOTES

1. Hanson, Melanie, "U.S. Public Education Spending Statistics," Education Data Initiative, June 15, 2022, https://educationdata.org/public-education-spending-statistics

2. Liscowski, Ola, "As K12 Education Funding Jumps Dramatically, Still Just 54% of Funding Spent on Instruction," *MacIver Institute*, March 5, 2020, https://www.maciverinstitute.com/2020/03/as-school-spending-rises-just-54-of-funding-spent-on-instruction

3. This number is their average for years 15 to 25 of this project.

4. This number is derived from data in table 14.1. Here's the math; $71,683 − 63,345 = \$6,329$. This wealth gain is a realization of the Andreas Schleicher quote already mentioned two times in this book. Here it is again: "The quality of schooling in a country is a reliable predictor of the wealth that country will produce in the long run." The argument fostered here is that most of the gain in Massachusetts is due to their superior schools. This also works for states.

5. Hanson, Kathryn, Stipek, Deborah, "Schools v. prisons: Education's the way to cut prison population," *Stanford Graduate School of Education,* May 16, 2014, https://ed.stanford.edu/in-the-media/schools-v-prisons-educations-way-cut-prison-population-op-ed-deborah-stipek

Chapter 17

What Changes Must Be Made to Reform the System?

This book concludes with a list of recommendations for change, things that will make a positive impact on the U.S. education system. Some of these have already been discussed as general topics in this book but others were not. This is not intended to be a final statement of what is needed to fix our ailing education system but is a good start.

The scope of this book is on the "big picture" issues. It does not consider such things as the best way to teach reading or math, and so forth. These topics are in the domain of the trained educator.

FIXES FOR THE SYSTEM

There are four "stand-out" reasons for the decline of our public schools. The first is parenting, the second is irresponsible management by school boards and superintendents, the third is runaway discipline problems, and the fourth is social promotion. After these four root causes are covered, many lesser, but still important issues, will be laid out.

Detailed Discussion of Proposals

1. Better Parenting

Fixing parenting is a huge challenge. It is not impossible, but some changes can be made. Most of you are great and loving parents, but there are large numbers of parents that may be loving but not careful enough in rearing their children.

If you latter parents are teaching your children respect and courtesy, empathy, and the value of education, this instruction is faltering while they are at school because many are disruptive children. Children who waste enormous amounts of classroom instruction time. This section is addressed to these parents. Here is some data that will smash the rosy, "all is okay" vision. There are some parents who do a poor job of nurturing their children. For example, 2017 was a high-water mark for Indiana (see table 16.1) where there were 33,979 cases filed of abuse. This data supports the contention that there are a lot of unsatisfactory parents in Indiana.[1]

Your author hears it quite often as teachers and parents are interviewed about how to fix our system. Teachers say, "I'd be okay if it weren't for the parents; some give me more trouble than their children." Many different studies and authors have all come to the same conclusion. It's the parents who are raising children who disrespect and degrade their teachers. This is equivalent to "eating your seed corn," you will make it through the winter but when spring comes there is nothing to plant.

Your children are misbehaving in school, showing disrespect for teachers, and wasting large blocks of instructional time cheating the students who are at school to learn. Your children are driving teachers away from teaching in huge numbers and when they are gone, what happens to your children? Schools can "fill in" with people off the street, but they are nowhere near the quality of a trained teacher.

There aren't enough religious or private schools to take up many more students. Many younger students who would like to dedicate their lives to making your children better people are no longer interested in teaching. Think about that, these people are being paid to help develop your children and can't do it because so many children act up, destroying large blocks of the precious 220 minutes.

Your children show disrespect by calling their teachers "bitch," "whore" or some other terrible names. They make fun of anything about other students or teachers they know will make them angry. You as parents must be showing contempt for schools and teachers and is it rubbing off on your children. Do you "stand up" for teachers at home? Do you explain to your children that teachers will be judging them and if they don't like it, CHANGE their behavior or level of effort? Just because teachers give a bad grade does not mean they don't like you; it means they are telling you to try harder, work harder, and develop a love of learning.

There is another aspect of education that is damaging the system, and that's parents who file lawsuits against teachers or schools at the slightest provocation. These lawsuits are warping school behavior in unreasonable ways. Teachers are told to "never touch a child, there is no such thing as a safe touch," meaning a lawsuit might get filed against the teacher.

Given the disrespect shown to teachers, parents are also looking for ways to "get back," to punish the teacher. After all, "my child is never wrong and I'm going to support them no matter what." These are kids, and they are wrong a lot; on the other hand, the teachers are trained professionals who can be wrong but not very often.

If you ever doubt that teachers are treated as described in this book, go to the website at elevateteachers.org and click on Lessons; select Lesson 4. You will find it hard to believe.

Can parents be held responsible for their disruptive child? See chapter 6 for this discussion.

2. School Boards and Superintendents Not Doing Their Job

In the field of business, there are clear lines of responsibility with associated compensation and accountability. If the business begins to falter, the board of directors must act; usually resulting in the termination of one or more top executives.

The school board has many responsibilities, but their primary job is to ensure a quality education for the students in their schools. The buck stops at the desk of the school board. It is their job to set and maintain high standards, keep them high, and require the students to meet the standards.

The "everybody gets a trophy" strategy is a losing strategy. On the other hand, they may be giving away higher grades to divert attention away from the unsatisfactory state of affairs in their schools.

Who cares if the students are awarded easy "A's"? It's a win-win deal all the way around, right? Not true. The easy "A's" demotivate the top students, and don't motivate the others to strive for improvement. Results of the U.S. Department of Education National Assessment of Educational Progress (NAEP) assessments make that clear; U.S. reading and math scores have not improved in 48 years. Easy "A's" aren't working.

America has 16,800 school districts with most likely a school board in each. Surely, these are not all working in concert to give away "A's." But they learn from each other, and all follow the same path. If they maintain high grading standards and their kids do not get into the colleges they desire because of lower grades, their school looks bad. University admittance departments are not naive, they know which schools' grade easy, and which are operating at a higher grading standard. When they admit students who do not require remediation, they know which school systems to favor.

Perhaps superintendents and school boards feel "boxed in" by union rules, state laws, or by financial restraints. If they could all organize under one flag and let the public know they are setting and enforcing high standards, they will win in their fight for their students' futures.

3. Runaway Discipline Problems Must Be Solved

Much time has been spent describing the discipline issue. Working teachers seldom publicly discuss their discipline problem because they feel responsible for it. The public sees this as one of their primary responsibilities and they do not want to admit they can't control their students. Be advised, the behavior of some of their children is well beyond their ability to control. Talk to a retired inner-city teacher and you will hear about the seriousness of the issue.

Some 80,000 U.S. schools are assessed to lose instruction time due to disruptive children.

The student discipline problem is due to many factors; some students live in an environment that is very tough on them and they must be tough to survive. Parenting plays a big role in how they are taught or not taught about profanity, respect, and so forth. One way to address this problem is to begin teaching character and grit/socio-emotional skills at age 3. This will fill in some of the gaps left by their parent's parenting style.

In chapter 6, this idea was introduced. Place all the disruptives in a separate class or better yet, a separate school. This at least gives the remaining teachers classes of children who can be taught. This also makes for happy teachers. Schools need to go out of their way to set up environments where teachers can do their jobs, educating children.

Make this statement a part of your disciplinary philosophy: *It is not allowed that one student will destroy the learning environment of another student.*

4. End Social Promotion

A child who is promoted to the fourth grade having not passed the reading requirement at the end of the third grade, has been socially promoted. The odds are very likely they *never* catch up. The social side of this decision to promote students is an important consideration, but it pales in importance to promoting a child who will never learn to read properly.

What is the general default policy supporting social promotions in today's schools? Figure 17.1 tells the story. (It was introduced in chapter 9.)

To better understand figure 17.1, look at the 2022 bar. Thirty-nine percent of *all* U.S. student reading test scores were "Below Basic," 29% performed at the "Basic" level, and so forth. Here's the important point. 39%

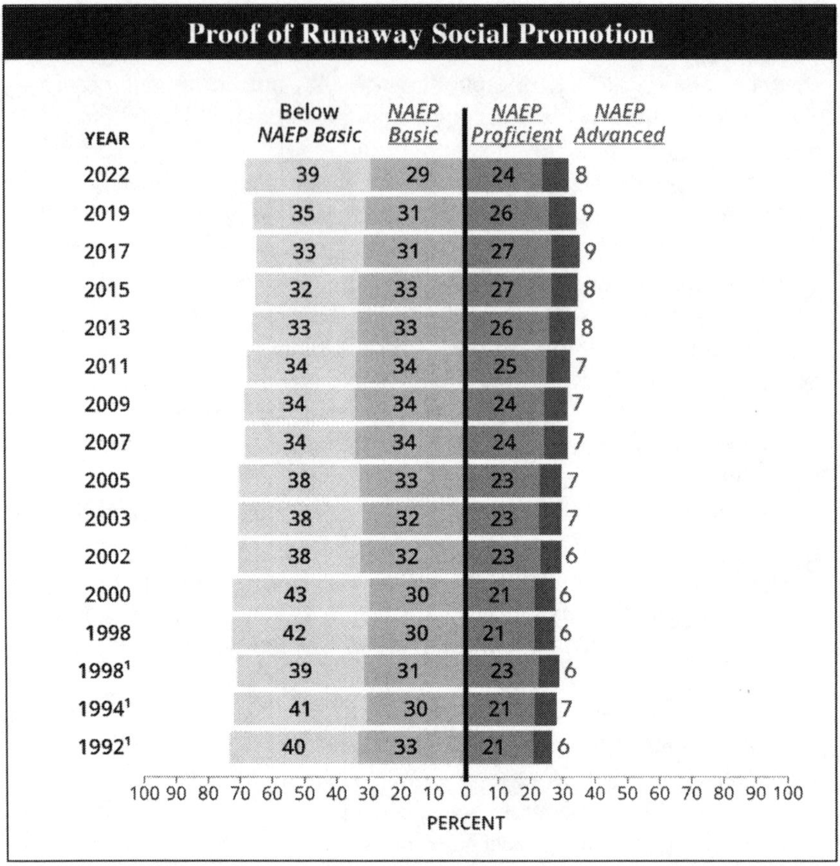

Proof of Runaway Social Promotion

YEAR	Below NAEP Basic	NAEP Basic	NAEP Proficient	NAEP Advanced
2022	39	29	24	8
2019	35	31	26	9
2017	33	31	27	9
2015	32	33	27	8
2013	33	33	26	8
2011	34	34	25	7
2009	34	34	24	7
2007	34	34	24	7
2005	38	33	23	7
2003	38	32	23	7
2002	38	32	23	6
2000	43	30	21	6
1998	42	30	21	6
1998[1]	39	31	23	6
1994[1]	41	30	21	7
1992[1]	40	33	21	6

100 90 80 70 60 50 40 30 20 10 0 10 20 30 40 50 60 70 80 90 100
PERCENT

Figure 17.1.   NAEP Reading Test Scores by Achievement Level

of the students in all U.S. fourth grades entered the grade unable to read at the proper level; they were all socially promoted! The assumption is that just a few months earlier, when they entered the fourth grade, they had the same level of reading ability as they had at the time they were tested.

Looking at *all the years* gives 37% as the average number of poor readers. For the entire nation this is about 2.2 million students. So, 2.2 million students are pushed forward into the education stream each year who most likely never become adequate readers. Is there evidence that this is happening? Yes, look back to chapter 2. Twenty-five percent of U.S. citizens (all high school graduates) ages 16 to 72 have the reading skills of a 10-year-old child. This is around 52 million citizens. So, there appears to be a general policy of promoting almost all students into the fourth grade regardless of the level of their reading skills.

The way to fix this problem is to develop a system that teaches every student how to read early on. This may mean that the schools have a cadre of reading experts or volunteers who step in to assist students who need extra help. The most foolproof method is to start developing their reading skills at ages 3 and 4, and develop their print concept skills before they enter kindergarten. Reading experts are employed to pull every student up to the proper level.

5. Forget the "Every Student Goes to College" Mantra

For years, the general philosophy for high schools has been to get each student college ready. The quality of a school system is often judged by how many students attend four-year universities upon graduation, the more prestigious college the better. This unrealistic goal distorts curriculum planning by dictating that all students pass classes that are not necessary if the students don't intend to go to college. For example, many high school graduates need go no further than middle school math to succeed in life and career.

In the good European systems, most students take the vocational/ technical route. Designing a curriculum that only a minority of students will need is not keeping up with the times. Our country needs more vocationally trained students to take the more technical industrial jobs.

6. Begin Formal Schooling at Three Years Old

Rather than go into a long discourse on early education you are referred to read chapter 10. Here are the main points to highlight:

- Starting children reading earlier can keep them from being socially promoted. Introducing them to the print concepts associated with books and reading gets them ready for kindergarten reading instruction.
- It is essential to begin brain stimulation during the peak years of zero to five years. They may not be getting this brain stimulation at home. If they miss it, they may never reach their genetic potential.
- Early education teaches social/emotional skills the student may not be getting at home.
- This begins to socialize the children and teaches them good manners and early noncognitive skills.
- Get them accustomed to the classroom routine.

7. Make Teachers Happy in Their Work

Many teachers go into the classroom with a mission to change student lives, to help them grow and acquire knowledge and skills they can use the rest of their lives. Many went into teaching because they admired and respected their own teachers.

Teachers want to be able to do their job, to use the full 220 minutes of instruction time. If that time is disrupted by unruly students, the teachers do not want to be held responsible for student test scores. Teachers do not want to be babysitters, which comes about when they are asked to take in students who have very little likelihood of learning.

How much should teachers be paid? The answer is simple: Pay them enough to get them to leave the general labor pool and work in the classroom. The Maryland Commission Study team determined this number was an average of $80,000. Teachers want to be empowered in their school and to be represented on the management team. This is a mark of a successful school. They want to be well managed and treated with respect by their leaders and students.

Teachers are getting paid to make our children more capable and better citizens. If we do not change the way they are treated, we will be seeing many empty classrooms or positions filled by taking in "people off the street." Consider that the projected 2025 shortfall of trained teachers is in the range of 200,000 out of a need for 300,000.

8. Develop a Career Path for Teachers

One of the characteristics of a teaching position is you start early in your life as a teacher and retire years later as a teacher. There is no career path. The Maryland study proposes a career ladder for teachers that places approximately 12% of a school's teacher staff into these three levels: Lead Teacher, Master Teacher, and Professor Master Teacher.

The ideal responsibility for the Professor Master Teacher is as a school's kaizen and quality control officer. The word *kaizen* is Japanese for "never-ending improvement." They will teach very little but will spend the bulk of their time working with teachers to improve the design and delivery of lessons, improve classroom management, and make all teachers better at what they do.

9. Empower Teachers

One sign of a well-managed school is empowered teachers. Teachers, or their representatives, who have a seat at the management table. This gives the teachers a direct voice and it shows that management wants to hear what they have to say. It elevates their stature.

10. Be Prepared to Expel Students

The idea of expulsion is difficult to discuss, but the discipline problem is so bad it is time for extreme measures. One of the keys to solving this problem is to identify the ringleaders, the "hard core" disruptives. They have already been put into one of the "all disruptive" classes but they continue to be a problem. This was their third strike; they are out. They must be expelled for an indefinite period until they are well behaved enough to remain in a classroom.

What about students' rights to an education? The U.S. Constitution does not consider education as an enumerated power. This leaves it to the states. Nonetheless, if a student, by their actions, *deprives the other students of their right to learn*, the rights of the offending student "fall away." This is a universal principle of law. Freedom of Speech, the First Amendment, is a fundamental right, but not if it interferes with the rights of others.

A little bit of this will go a long way. Other students will see the school will no longer tolerate abhorrent behavior and it will impact them if they do.

11. Foster the Return of Consequences

There is no better way to force a student to face the consequences of their action than expulsion. Where do they go for the next year? They should be enrolled in some type of "boot camp" where strong leadership is exerted to get them to be better citizens. It is hard to say why schools are inclined to forgive and forget so many infractions. Could it be the preservation of self-esteem discussed in chapter 3? Could it be the avoidance of lawsuits? Could it be they are doing the student a favor to foster a relationship?

Whatever the reason, it is not real life, and it does not teach the student anything but how to get away with bad behavior. Chapter 3 discusses an article in a 2004 issue of *Psychology Today* titled, "The Gift of Failure, Letting Our Children Struggle Is a Difficult Gift to Give." The article points out that people must all learn to deal with setbacks and failures. The logic being none of the failures of youth are of much significance. A person develops resilience, the ability to get off the floor and keep on living, the ability to learn from failure and to avoid the situation again.

12. Students Must Pass Their Final Assessment Exam in Order to Graduate

There are two ways to design a school curriculum: (1) U.S. schools fix the time and accept the level of knowledge accumulated by the students, or (2) fix the knowledge requirement and vary the time. This latter method seems superior, but varying the time would create huge management issues.

Asking students to pass the final assessment exam in 10th or 12th grade makes the school program into a blend to both methods. It is a fixed period with an acquired knowledge of adequate depth to pass the exam. Simply passing the exam does not seem like much of a hurdle, but it's a start. Once the system has adjusted, more can be demanded later.

This is an excellent place to execute consequences. Meaning, if the students do not measure up to the mark, they do not receive a diploma. There is no certificate of attendance, no substandard document saying they tried. They MUST meet certain minimal requirements for accumulated knowledge to graduate.

13. Set High Standards and Stick with Them

Find success stories in the newspapers or magazine articles and the common factor in most of them is high standards. Don't "dumb down" the work; set high standards and demand that the students rise to the occasion. What kind of a standard delivers "A's" to 47% of high schoolers? What kind of standards allow schools to select 117 students to be valedictorians? These are examples of the discredited practice of giving everybody a trophy.

Eenforcement must be consistent across the state. Assign the state school board and state superintendent of education as the place that sets and maintains standards for schools. This keeps local school board members from facing political backlash from tighter grading and other more stringent policies, such as having only one class valedictorian.

14. Accelerate Learning to Reduce the Teaching of the Common Core to 10 Years Instead of 12

In the best international systems, the teaching of the "Common Core" is reduced for most students from 12 years to 10 years. This leaves two years of high school that is devoted to two things, depending on which track the student selects. For university-bound students it is for advanced placement courses to allow the student to pick up large numbers of college credits while still in high school. For vocational students, it should provide time for them to earn industry-certified certificates for their selected skill.

15. Set Up a Four Track System for High Schools

One of the keys to a successful system is "everyone has a track." In this scheme many students will probably select track 3. This is how it works in most advanced international systems. Once a student can visualize a place for them to do what they want to do, motivation builds.

As was pointed out earlier, our interests are to educate individuals, not groups. There is a belief that by mixing strong students with weaker students, the overall class average will be elevated. This is not the right idea; it is a good example of the convoy speed being set by the speed of the slowest ship. What is needed is multiple convoys, each traveling at their own speed.

Notice tracks 3 and 4. These tracks have a reduced math requirement. As was pointed out earlier, many of us can go through life and be successful if we know middle school math. This concept will make these tracks more appealing because many folks do not like math and are dreading high school math because it does not seem relevant to them. Is this dumbing down education? Not really; there are many things not taught in school that have value, but if they are not relevant, they are excluded. High school math is relevant for the students going on to a university, and they will get their math.

A needed attribute of a system like this is mobility between tracks. If a student on track 2 believes they belong on track 1 they can "test

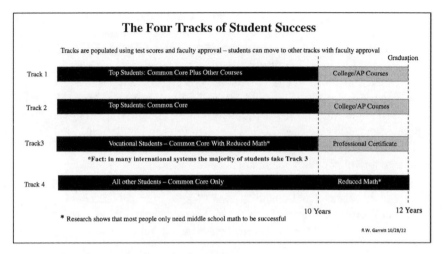

Figure 17.2. The Four Tracks to Student Success

the water" by moving onto that track to see if they can do the work. A similar logic exists on the other tracks.

16. Reduce High School Math for Some Students

The math curriculum for most high schools has been established to prepare students to enter a university. Since only a minority attend a university, reduce the math requirement for students not headed for college. The more appropriate level would be middle school math. Looking at the four-track proposal shown above, only tracks 1 and 2 have the more complex math requirement.

17. Reduce the Chances for a Lawsuit

The threat of or actual filing of lawsuits dramatically changes the game for schools. Every touch, every bad grade, every disciplinary action and so forth can turn into a lawsuit. Schools must defend themselves by documenting their procedures, teaching employees how and when to engage a process, then documenting what happened with the student. "Never touch a child" is not a law but a policy decision because experience teaches, "there is no such thing as a safe touch."

This is a perplexing issue. All an American needs to file a lawsuit against anybody is some paperwork and a filing fee. For Indiana, the filing fees vary depending upon the nature of the suit but $150 to $175 will cover most filings. This is not a high hurdle and will not be a burden to most people. Americans have grown more litigious, filing lots of lawsuits against schools. Of course, most people will need to engage an attorney to fill out the paperwork and follow the rules.

An example: a parent might sue a school because the school sent their child home to change from immodest clothing to something more modest.

This upsets the parents, after all they saw what the child was wearing and tacitly approved it by not forcing the child to change their outfit.

When the school overrides their decision, they rise up and file a lawsuit. By most definitions, this is a trivial matter that should not be resolved in court. The only person who can officially make that call is a judge, but putting the case in front of a judge means the school district must engage an attorney. This costs money, and there are many lawsuits.

18. Ensure Education Has a Good ROI (Return on Investment)

This is not like the other ideas listed but it is a reminder. Every student who graduates with intellectual or technical skills (vocational) gets a well-paying job and pays taxes. Looking at Indiana as an example, the state graduates about 66,000 students a year from public schools. As Bill Gates reminds, about 30% of the students dropped out before graduation. This means 94,000 started their journey and never completed it, at least in the usual 12 years. This is a loss of 28,000 potential employees.

The CCR rate in Indiana is about 35% so another 43,000 are not attractive university or trade school candidates and therefore not good employee material. This is a total loss of 71,000 potential employees. This is a huge number; it overstates the case because many of these folks will "wise up" and find a path to some sort of economic success.

Here's the point; had they stayed in school many of these people would be employed in well-paying jobs paying state and federal taxes. Also, some of the dropouts would have ended up on government support (food stamps, rent and energy assistance, Medicaid, etc.). Some would end up being incarcerated with an associated large annual cost to the governments. These now employed folks are saving taxpayer money since they are not on the government programs.

Additional intangible benefits accrue to society. Both economic and social stature are enhanced with a better educated public. A better-educated populace will produce a better democracy.

19. Teacher Labor Unions

This expression comes to mind when thinking about unions: "Lead, follow or get out of the way." What will union folks say about these recommended changes? If history is correct, they will fight many of them "to the extremes." Massachusetts is a strong union state, yet they enacted the Education Reform Act of 1993. How did the unions react to this change?

First, when it comes to state policy, the Massachusetts teachers' unions have been remarkably weak over the past fifteen years. They accepted the 1993 reform bill, as it came attached to hundreds of millions of dollars in new spending. But from all accounts it appears that they thought they'd be able to delete the reform elements over time.

And they tried, battling the standards, the tests, the accountability, the higher standards for new teachers, the charter schools, everything. And time and again, they lost. That's partly because Massachusetts had (an improbable) string of Republican governors in the 1990s and 2000s, and that's partly because of reform-minded Democratic legislators (like Tom Birmingham). And now that a Democrat has taken over the governor's chair, the union is starting to get its way.[2]

This quotation leads one to believe that the Massachusetts Miracle might not have happened if the unions were under a Democratic governor. This again illustrates the way unions resist improvements in the education of our children.

Do they acknowledge that our education system is in trouble? Do they see a huge teacher shortage coming? Do they think we're in a crisis? Where is their list of needed changes? Would it say all will be better with more union influence? Where has this union influence helped in the past? Having to spend thousands of dollars and years of wasted time keeping the worst of the teachers employed has not been helpful. If they are not going to help solve our problems and they will not follow our lead, then get out of the way. These are serious issues, and we don't have time to spare.

A recommendation to the unions. The ideas presented in this book will make life more pleasant and valuable for teachers. It will provide a classroom environment that will allow them to do their primary task, teach students. This will improve morale and make the classroom job more appealing to young people so they will be willing to become teachers.

Unions are certainly respected advisories, are well organized, have good people, show lots of passion, and are politically adroit. They have political power. Join the team to pursue educational excellence, and with your help wonderful things will be accomplished making us a better nation and a more competitive international player in the task of creating wealth in this country.

20. Beware of Runaway Overhead

More money needs to flow to teachers; keep this in mind when funding spectacular athletic facilities. Consolidate administrative offices down to one per county in smaller counties. In the larger cities find ways to consolidate school administrators and thereby reduce overhead.

21. Attract Many New Students into Teaching

Teacher supply is approaching huge shortfalls relative to need. Many of these reform proposals require additional teachers to implement. It is imperative to increase pay and "fix the classrooms" very quickly. Fixing the classroom means the teachers have needed minutes to teach each day; this along with stronger support from the principal's office, will allow them to "do their job." This is what it takes to attract new candidates into the ranks of teaching, reasonable pay, and a chance to teach!

22. Teachers Are Not Babysitters

If a student has only a very small likelihood of being able to learn they do not belong in the classroom. Teachers have a critically important job to teach the students who want to and can learn. Do not turn a teacher into a babysitter; focus all their energies on teaching.

IN CONCLUSION

This book has presented a bleak picture of the U.S. education system, but it has also presented ideas of how to fix it. Is there any reason for hope? Absolutely. The 22 ideas presented will go a long way toward the creation of an excellent system. In and of themselves, not all these ideas are solutions.

For example, look at social promotion. The book points out that essentially *all* third-grade students are socially promoted. Fixing this problem will require a lot of study. How much impact will starting some students at 3 years old have on this problem? How can summers be used to set up reading camps for those that need more instruction? The objective is to put all third-grade students in a position where they can be successful passing the reading exams. This will end social promotion and will have a huge impact on student performance in later grades. How much will this cost? It will most likely be expensive, but reading is a fundamental skill. All students must be able to read!

Here is a plan of action to begin serious reform. As was pointed out in chapter 11, the most prominent vested interest is in the business community. All business folks are concerned about where they will find good future employees. Look to the state chambers of commerce to take the lead role. They should establish state educational reform commissions that would use this book as a guide to direct their actions.

NOTES

1. Children in Need of Services, Indiana Department of Child Services.
2. Petrilli, Michael J., "What Does the Massachusetts Miracle Teach Us About Teacher Unions?," Thomas Fordham Institute, May 18, 2009, https://fordhaminstitute .org/national/commentary/what-does-massachusetts-miracle-teach-us-about-teachers -unions

Appendix

Introduction to Website

The focus of this appendix is to highlight "Lessons on Education" that are a part of the website: elevateteachers.org.

Several years ago, the author created a "web-based book" that would be multimedia and feature "Lesson on Education." Each lesson would be equivalent to a chapter of a conventional book. Each lesson is a stand-alone Power Point session with many embedded videos. A total of 27 lessons were created and several more are planned, but these latter lessons would be created after reader volume increased. Sadly, not enough people found these lessons so further development was stopped.

Below is the Table of Contents for all 27 lessons and a present brief description of each.

Figure A.1. Home Page of Website elevateteachers.org

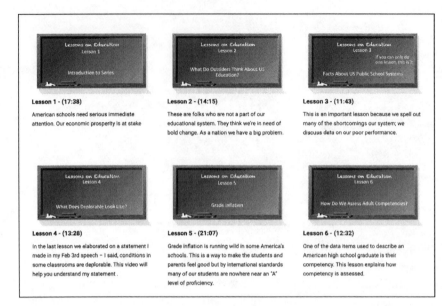

Lesson 1 - (17:38)
American schools need serious immediate attention. Our economic prosperity is at stake

Lesson 2 - (14:15)
These are folks who are not a part of our educational system. They think we're in need of bold change. As a nation we have a big problem.

Lesson 3 - (11:43)
This is an important lesson because we spell out many of the shortcomings our system; we discuss data on our poor performance.

Lesson 4 - (13:28)
In the last lesson we elaborated on a statement I made in my Feb 3rd speech – I said, conditions in some classrooms are deplorable. This video will help you understand my statement .

Lesson 5 - (21:07)
Grade inflation is running wild in some America's schools. This is a way to make the students and parents feel good but by international standards many of our students are nowhere near an "A" level of proficiency.

Lesson 6 - (12:32)
One of the data items used to describe an American high school graduate is their competency. This lesson explains how competency is assessed.

Figure A.2.   First Page of Lessons, 27 Lessons Total

TABLE OF CONTENTS:

Lesson Descriptions

Lesson 1: Introduction

An introduction to this series of lessons and the assessment of when and why the U.S. began its downward spiral in public education. This lesson features a video of the TV host Steve Harvey as he explains why every kid doesn't need a trophy.

Lesson 2: Some Outside Opinions

Three outsiders express concern about the state of U.S. education. This is an excellent opportunity to hear from Marc Tucker who is one of the experts on how to bring the best of top foreign systems to our U.S. schools.

Lesson 3: Facts about the U.S. Public School System

This is an excerpt taken from the author's February 3, 2020, talk given to the Indianapolis Scientech Club.

Lesson 4: What Does Deplorable Look Like?

In the previous lessons, the comment was made that in many classrooms the behavior of the students can be deplorable. This video gives a vivid look at why this expression is used.

Lesson 5: Grade Inflation

Forty-seven percent of U.S. high schoolers carry an "A" average. This has negative implications for several things, and this lesson elaborates on some of these negative implications. These results were for both public and private schools.

Lesson 6: The Assessment of Adult Competency

Some of the most damning data about the poor training U.S. public high school students demonstrate comes from the Program for the International Assessment of Adult Competencies. The purpose of this lesson is to get the reader comfortable with this assessment program.

Lesson 7: Teacher Shortages

The current projection for teacher needs and teacher supply (Prof. Linda Darling-Hammond of Stanford University) show a huge shortfall in the immediate future. In fact, the need is projected to be 300,000 trained teachers and a supply of only 100,000.

Lesson 8: Who's Gonna Fix This Problem?

This lesson discusses why the solutions to the educational problems we are covering in these lessons will most likely not come from within the school system. Most likely it will begin with some outside business organization, such as the state chamber of commerce, political groups like state school boards or education committees, and so on.

Lesson 9: The Author's Book

The book, *The Kids Are Smart Enough, So What's the Problem?* was released in December of 2017. This lesson highlights some of the findings from the book. The most important thing this book does is to quantify the amount of lost instructional time that can result from disruptive students. A common-sense result: if a teacher is disciplining children they are not teaching!

Lesson 10: 80,000 Schools

In 2004, the think tank Public Agenda published a report titled *Teaching Interrupted.* The title refers to the lost instruction time associated with misbehaving children. They survey teachers and parents and conclude that about 80% of all public-school classrooms lose time because of the behavior of their disruptive children.

Lesson 11: Motivation

Intrinsic motivation is the ideal way to motivate children. This lesson discusses the importance of reaching a high motivational level using methods that foster intrinsic motivation.

Lesson 12: Reading 1

Reading, reading, reading, it's all about reading. In grades K-3 a child learns to read, then from grade 4 and beyond they use their reading skills to learn. If a child cannot read by the end of the third grade, their educational future is in jeopardy; most likely they will never catch up.

Lesson 13: Reading 2

More on reading.

Lesson 14: Social Promotion

Social promotion is not academic promotion. Kids are moved forward to the next grade without regard as to whether they have the requisite skills. Holding a child back has social implications that may interfere with their socialization. On the other hand, moving them forward, say into the fourth grade, when they cannot read at grade level, has serious academic implications. Most likely they will never overcome this shortfall.

Lesson 15: How to Improve PISA Scores

The Program for International Student Assessment (PISA) is used in approximately 80 countries to monitor how students are progressing. Tests of 15-year-old students are given every three years. The main areas for the exams are reading, mathematics, and science. U.S. students in the *top two quartiles* of socioeconomic standing perform as well as any country. Where the U.S. falls behind is in the education of the bottom two quartiles.

Lesson 16: Educating Our Less Fortunate

This lesson focuses on the education of the bottom two socioeconomic quartiles of U.S. students. By one measure, if we could improve test scores for the bottom quartile by 8%, we would be much more competitive.

Lesson 17: The Massachusetts Success Story

In 1993, the state of Massachusetts was forced to equalize spending across all schools. This reform produced marvelous results putting the state atop all U.S. public-school systems.

Lesson 18: The Harlem Children's Zone

Geoffrey Canada's Harlem Children's Zone is a major triumph. After many years of experimentation, he finally discovered a successful process to get his children educated and into college.

Lesson 19: The Maryland Move to World Class

Born of a desire to hold their position as one of the best state systems in the U.S., Maryland commissioned a team to make a proposal that would position them as a world-class state. It is an excellent study of what it takes and how much it costs to be world class. It is a work-in-progress.

Lesson 20: The Role of Character

Students possessing character and grit will be better behaved in class and graduate as better citizens. Our school systems must produce good scholars who are good citizens. Character and grit can be taught.

Lesson 21: The White-Black Gap Is Closing

There is evidence that the widely publicized shortfall of black test scores is slowly closing. This lesson will discuss this gap and where it is beginning to improve.

Lesson 22: Teaching the Poor—How to Do It Right

One of the things you learn when you study school systems with top-tier programs in other countries is that they have as many poor children in their classes as we do in the United States. One of the differences between us is their allocation of extra funding to properly educate these poor children. In fact, they begin at 3 years old to capture as much of the vital first five years of development of a child's brain as possible.

Lesson 23: Does Early Learning Fade Away?

There is data that supposedly illustrates that early learning (ages 3+) doesn't pay off because by the end of the third grade you can no longer differentiate the early learners. There is other data that refutes this finding. This lesson discusses the impact of early learning.

Lesson 24: Teachers—A Video Montage

What are the most important factors in the success of a school? Here are three of the first six: teachers, teachers, teachers. You cannot have an excellent educational program without excellent teachers.

Lesson 25: Teachers—The State of the Profession

This chapter discusses some of the factors that are in play as the satisfaction of our teacher corps is assessed. For the most part, many, many teachers are unhappy, and many will leave the profession.

Lesson 26: Teachers—Life in a Top-Tier System

If you were a teacher in a top-tier system, such as Finland, you would be an outstanding student, but that alone won't necessarily get you the job. You would be well paid and respected, and you can teach; the students will behave and listen.

Lesson 27: Teacher Unions

There are many factors in the creation of a first-class school system. Teacher unions are the biggest determent to school excellence. Teachers should be represented by a union but not the kind of unions that now exist. With all their strong leadership and political power, they could do wonders to help America reach educational excellence.

Index

Page numbers in italics refer to figures and tables.

workers: blue-collar, 75; in schools, *xvii*, xvii–xix; white-collar, 75

Yankelevich, Daniel, 41
Yeager, Lee, 99

Young, Paul, 99
Youngstown, 81
youth sports, 15–16

zest, 63

About the Author

Richard W. Garrett has been engaged in research on educational reform since 2013.

This is the second major literary effort for this author. Prior to this book, his most significant publication was the book *The Kids Are Smart Enough, So What's the Problem? A Businessman's Perspective on Educational Reform and the Teacher Crisis*, published by Rowman & Littlefield, December 2017. Another notable effort was an article in the *Harvard Business Review*, titled "Weighing Risk in Capacity Expansion."

The author is a trained industrial engineer, BS and MS (Purdue), and has a PhD in operations research (Northwestern University). He also attended DePauw University for two years before transferring to Purdue. He has 27 years of business experience with Eli Lilly and Company, a large pharmaceutical company.

Beginning in 1994, having retired from Lilly, he was an associate clinical professor at the Kelley School of Business, Indiana University, Bloomington, and during the same period he was a partner in a consulting firm. During his six and one-half years at IU he won an award for the most Innovative New Course in the MBA program. During 10 years of his working career, he served as an accreditor of engineering departments around the country through ABET.

During his years at Eli Lilly, he was one of the corporate leaders in the use of the Total Quality process and was an expert in supply chain management. He has facilitated approximately 60 long-range plans for nonprofit groups in central Indiana. He is the founder of the website www.elevateteachers.org.